LIVING LIFE AS A PRAYER

LIVING LIFE AS A PRAYER

a guide to healing and wholeness

CAROL MARCY, PH.D.

To order additional copies of this book, contact:
Xlibris Corporation
1-888-795-4274
www.Xlibris.com
Orders@Xlibris.com
27626

CONTENTS

Dedicated to Cynthia and Tyler Marcy.

ACKNOWLEDGEMENTS

Creator of All Things, I am grateful for the words that have flowed onto the pages of this book and that now become available for others to read. May they be supportive and beneficial. If it had not been for the encouragement of the Council of ADRON and my sister, Starfeather, I would never have even begun the endeavor of putting down my experiences on paper. At the beginning of this work, I used to say, "I hardly ever read books, how can I begin to write one." With time and effort that has all changed. At the Council's continued nudging, I now call myself a writer. I am grateful for the help of Peter Porosky, who took my eighth grade English and taught me how to construct a good English sentence. My friend Phebe Barth took the time to read what I was writing in detail and made very helpful suggestions.

I am grateful for my teachers Sings Alone in the Night, Buffalo Protects Her and White Horse Woman, who initiated me onto the Native American spiritual path, for Clyde Hall and all of the elders of the Naraya, who give much of their time and wisdom to keep the dance alive. I thank Rudy Bauer and the Wednesday morning seminar group. They keep coming back with discipline and love to hold the Field and explore levels of higher consciousness. This safe powerful pool of loving energy has allowed me to dive in deep and flood my being with growing states of ecstasy and God consciousness until these places are alive and well in my experience consistently. I am grateful for Dr. Eric Pearl and the Reconnection. This way of working with energy and light has been an incredible gift. Tom Kenyon and Judy Sion have opened doorways through sound, energy and healing that have allowed me to go deeper and bring more to my work.

I give many thanks to my clients from whom I have learned a tremendous amount. Their generosity and willingness to share their stories has greatly enriched this book. My children, Alyosha and Marin have taught me more than anyone, making me examine myself, because of what I saw reflected in them. It is a joy to love them so completely and to watch the Great Mystery unfold within them as adults. My sisters Jane and Barbara and my father Tyler have supported me with much love. I honor my mother, Cynthia for all she gave to me, like sitting for long hours in very boring dance recitals when I was a child. I am very grateful for all that has been created in my life.

I am grateful for our Mother the Earth, who has given me a place to call home. I thank you for this beautiful place I am given to live, learn and play. Thank you for the ring of crystals who keep this place sacred and holy, for the trees who provide this green cathedral within which I live, for my animals who provide such love and companionship, for the wild things who surround me and move through me, for all of the Devas and Nature Spirits who dance for joy all around this place. I send my love.

Thank you for life itself: the joy and struggle and learning that have occurred in the process of creating this book and the stories that fill it.

Ho, Mitakuye Oyasin!

Hello Divine Oneness
We are gathered here within you,
this special group of beings.
We thank you for this day.
We thank you for each other.
I thank you for me.
We dedicate this day to the
honor and purpose of oneness.
We ask that everything
we need be provided for.
We ask that everything
we do today, say today,
and hear today be only
in the highest good,
in my highest good,
in the highest good for all concerned
for all of life and everywhere
throughout the universe.

Traditional Australian Aborigine Morning Greeting

INTRODUCTION

You are a prayer that is offered every moment of every day to God and all of life everywhere. Every word you speak, action you take, and feeling you express becomes part of the prayer that you construct with your life. The purpose of this book is to help you to construct that prayer consciously.

Living Life as a Prayer invites you to create and manifest a way of life that honors your natural state of being. This natural way is to live in the flow of the grace of *divine energy* and to move into the world from the place of a loving heart. Your loving heart not only embraces other people and all of life but yourself as well. It has been said, "Love yourself enough to love another." You are the prayer that is being offered to the Great Mystery, to the unnamed force that runs through all of life. You are the healing force in the universe. A bumper sticker reads, "World peace begins at home." Home is in your own heart. You have the power to bring peace to the world by creating peace in your own heart. Part of the process of becoming a living prayer that you are comfortable with and happy to manifest is to learn to open your heart without fear.

How do you become a conscious living prayer? One way is to weave the sacred into your daily life. Each of us has a body, mind, and spirit that are not separated one from the other. Conceptualize yourself as a rich tapestry that is being woven from all of the threads of your experiences: red, gold, green, a touch of purple here, and a thread of silver there. When you bring together the full truth of who you are, you experience wholeness and sacredness. Prayer is a constant living thing.

To think of your life as a prayer is one way to draw all of these threads together. It doesn't just happen on Sunday morning or every night before you go to bed. By becoming increasingly aware of every thought you initiate, every word you speak, every feeling that rises up and every action you make, you begin to consciously construct the living prayer that you are. By living consciously, you become more vitally alive, more radiant, and more loving. Living in this manner, you are so much more capable of contributing something positive to all of life just by being who you are.

On the one hand, this process is very simple, and on the other hand, it is very complex. It is simple because it is about expanding your awareness and remembering to be grateful for the *divine love* that is in constant exchange between yourself and all of life everywhere. Because this exchange is always going on, it is simply a question of taking the time to become aware of it and embrace it. It is complex because it is challenging to be open and loving, cleanly

15

and clearly, without a lot of your own personal "gunk" getting in the way. While living this life as a student in "Earth School," you can choose to let go of the gunk and heal in order to become aligned with your higher nature and move the seat of your consciousness to your heart. You can choose to see your mistakes and failures as part of the lessons that you are learning on this path of rediscovering your intimate connection with the divine life force. You are here to learn how to get out of your own way in order to become your natural self again. By opening up the doors of the heart to the *divine energy* within and all around us, you have the opportunity to shine your unique and beautiful self out into the world.

The Native American people say that there are many paths to the Sacred Mountain, where one finds the Creator/God alive and well within. In other words, there is no one right way to find God within. There are many, many tools that are available to help you on this journey toward wholeness and well-being. Part of the task is learning to go slowly enough to smell the roses, to move into a place of inner silence so that you can tune into your own inner guidance, to feel your own intuitive impulses, and to learn the language of your own creative spirit. Creating your own personal journey and honoring your individual process helps you open to your own god-self. This enables you to carry the *divine light* of peace and love and become a vibrant part of the healing force in the universe.

Living Life as a Prayer is one of those tools. As practical guide, specific processes are offered with clear steps that can be taken to participate in them. Each of these is illustrated by wonderful stories from my own experience and from the experiences of others. The sections are also full of beautiful prayers from a number of different traditions. Because I live a Native American spirituality, there are a number of examples from that rich tradition. You will find the *divine energy* that connects all things into one unity of love referred to in a number of ways: God, the Creator, the Great Mystery, the Universal Life Force, the Universe, All that Is, Divine Light, Christ consciousness. This is done to help you expand your own personal vision of "the Divine."

Living Life as a Prayer is created in two parts. The first section focuses on preparing yourself to become the prayer. Here you will find healing techniques discussed and illustrated.These techniques will help you clear the way. By learning to remove the internal "gunk," you begin to open to the Divine within, become familiar and comfortable with expressing your feelings, and discover your own beauty. When I refer to "beauty" in this way, I am referring to the Navaho concept of walking in beauty. This is another way to speak about being in alignment with the Divine by recognizing and connecting to the beauty and love within you and the beauty and love that surrounds you. This alignment facilitates your living in divine flow, which means manifesting the grace of divine will, or walking in beauty.

The second section teaches how to create the living prayer and make it manifest in your daily life. Learning to structure both verbal and nonverbal prayers helps you to bring them into your daily routine and ensure a positive, abundant way of thinking about life. Learning to move into the silence allows you to open up the guidance within. When you begin to open up to inner as well as other sources of guidance, it becomes very important to learn to discern the true voice. You are given some guidelines to help you with discernment. You will also be taught how to use rituals in your daily life and during special occasions. Rituals help us recognize and magnify the presence of the Divine in all things. As you open more and more to the forces of the Divine, there will come a time when you will ask yourself to be available to God. By letting go of your own desire to control everything, you will learn how to allow yourself to go with the divine flow: to trust the "God force" in you and you in the "God force."

What we do is not for ourselves alone. The energy that comes from the choices you make in living your life is the same as the waves emanating out from a pebble thrown into a large pond. Those waves ripple out all the way to the edge. As others throw in their pebbles, your ripples affect theirs just as theirs will affect yours. The pond is the universe, and your ripples are felt to the far reaches of outer space. How do you choose to create and manifest those ripples? consciously or unconsciously? with awareness or without?

Living Life as a Prayer will support you in developing a process that will bring your life into a consciously prayerful way of being in alignment with your higher nature. In the past, we have looked to the holy men and women to be the mediums through which we converse with God. We are now in a time when walking in a sacred manner is not just for the mystic or the hermit on the mountain but for everyone—you and me. All are being called upon to develop the capacity to carry the *divine light* in our daily lives. In the past, we have asked to be healed or saved as if God were a force outside of ourselves. The time has come to embrace the Great Spirit within. It is your job to lift the veils from your eyes and experience the fullness of who you are as *divine light*. As you learn to manifest this experience in the world, you become part of the healing force that moves into the universe. You become a very important instrument of peace and love by the way you talk, think, act, and feel, every moment of every day.

PART I

Preparing Yourself to Become a Living Prayer

CHAPTER I

Setting an Intention

"What if you slept,
And what if,
in your sleep
you dreamed?
And what if,
in your dream,
you went to heaven
and there plucked
a strange and beautiful flower?
And what if,
when you awoke,
you had the flower
in your hand?
What then?"

Deepak Chopra[1]

1. Setting an Intention to Heal

A few years ago, I set the intention to learn more about how to restore balance and harmony to the whole person after an experience of trauma. I had been inspired by an account of healing done by an aboriginal group in Australia that was described by Marlo Morgan in her book *Mutant Message Down Under.*[2]

In late January, I put my intention in the form of a prayer, when I spent the night in the Sweat Lodge[3] after a Native American purification ceremony. If I

---

[1]   Deepak Chopra, *The Way of the Wizard: Twenty Spiritual Lessons for Creating the Life You Want* (New York: Harmony Books, 1995), p. 52.

[2]   Marlo Morgan, *Mutant Message Down Under: A Woman's Journey into Dreamtime Australia,* (New York: HarperCollins, 1995).

[3]   The Sweat Lodge is a small round hut built in a prescribed manner and covered with blankets. It is the womb of the Grandmother Earth within whom we come to pray and purify.

had any expectation about the way the learning would unfold, I thought maybe it would come through my work with clients. I am a clinical psychologist and have the opportunity to work with people, some of whom have been severely traumatized.

The universe had something else in mind.

That spring, on the equinox, I went to the West Coast. A medicine woman from the White Horse family of the Cherokee people was doing a Walk into the Grandmother Lodge ceremony[4] for my sister and myself. After this incredible ceremony, we went off to LaPush, a Quillieut Indian reservation, on the Pacific Coast. My sister, Starfeather, was leading a Shield Building retreat[5].

It was cold and drizzling when we arrived. I made my way down to the beach by climbing over huge logs three to four feet in diameter where they had been tossed up on shore by storms. I had a feeling that I might fall, so I was moving cautiously. I made my prayers of thanks for the beautiful ceremony, for all who had had a hand in making it happen and for my safe arrival. I gave special greetings to the Devas and Nature Spirits, who create and care for this enchanted place. On my way back over the logs, I found myself standing about four feet off the ground. I have an extensive background in modern dance and know my body pretty well, but this time, I jumped off onto one leg instead of two.

Strange!

My left knee went screaming out to one side, tearing ligaments when it could not support my weight. As I fell to the ground, I knew somehow that this was part of the lesson that I had asked to learn. In order to counter the waves of panic that were sweeping over me, I wrapped my shawl tightly around my shoulders, lay on the damp earth, held my knee with both hands, and prayed to her to hold me and help heal me. Then I began to sing and hum to my knee to calm down and realign the energetic patterns of shock and injury back to healthy energetic lines. As the waves of panic subsided, my mind stopped spinning. I lay there for as long as it took to get centered and grounded. I had not known how to do this ahead of time. It was unfolding in that moment.

I pulled myself up onto my good leg. Our cabins faced the beach, and women were arriving for the weekend workshop. They caught my signal and came to carry me off the beach. A friend, who was a Reiki[6] practitioner, put her

---

4   The Walk into the Grandmother Lodge Ceremony, performed by a medicine woman within a community of women, tests, initiates, and honors a holy woman who has not menstruated for at least a year and who has chosen to serve her people.

5   Starfeather's Shield Building Retreat is held on the equinox for the purpose of enhancing spiritual growth and development. As part of the process, a circular shield is created by each participant as a symbolic representation of her personal journey.

6   Reiki is an ancient form of Japanese hands on energy healing that has been recently rediscovered.

hands on my knee. As people gathered around, I asked for my rattle. Following an inner impulse, I requested that people begin to hum, and a healing ceremony spun itself into being.

Later, sitting in circle, processing the experience, we discovered that it was the humming that helped the women to know their place in the healing dance. Those who had arrived with aches and pains from a long drive or a hard week reported that they too felt soothed and cared for. The next day, I was a little disappointed that I was not up and walking like the way it had happened in the Aboriginal story, but I figured that I was not a trained and practiced Aboriginal healer either. I was going to have to give up my ideas of hiking through the Hoh Rainforest or along the crest of the Olympic range. I was going to have to sit quietly and "be" instead of "do." What a concept! With the help of flower essences, love and care from my sister, the stone people and cedar people, rest and a knee brace, at the end of the week, I was walking easily and carrying my heavy luggage through the airport.

A few weeks later, I felt the nudge of my inner voice suggesting that I go for a walk in the woods. The ground was very uneven, so I put on the brace for safekeeping and went to a spot where I had constructed a simple medicine wheel[7] of five stones. The medicine wheel is a Native American construct that symbolizes all of life and its interrelatedness. Being out among the trees again felt very good. I really love the trees, but I had been playing it safe and staying on level ground. After prayers of gratitude were expressed to each of the four directions, I simply sat on the soft forest floor. I must have been there for longer than I thought, because the light began to fade. Starting back a different way, I remembered that I had left my glasses at the base of a large beech tree. Once they were retrieved, I made a straight line for home.

As I was walking along, all of a sudden, my left foot went into a hole, and I lost my balance. My knee bent severely. I yelled out from the pain and then got angry. I was out in the woods because I had been guided to be here, but now look what had happened. It wasn't fair. I vented my anger to God. When I calmed down, I noticed a white spider on my left shoe. It caught my eye because of its unusual color and because it didn't budge when I moved to sit up. Spiders remind me of fate because I see their beautifully and intricately woven webs and I'm reminded of the complex web of life. Was it fate that I had fallen? Maybe there was a purpose in it. I called out. A friend had just come outside my house and heard me. He made his way out through the woods by following my voice. He helped me walk across the stream and up a very steep hill. By the time we

---

[7]   The medicine wheel is a Native American construction that has a very specific design that represents the Creator, the moon cycles of the year, and every aspect of creation. Some of its uses are as a calendar and a tool for journey or meditation.

reached the top, my hobbling had stopped, and I was walking far better than before.

Later, when I drove with a friend out to a Good Medicine Society[8] gathering, I told my story. He suggested that often, when there is an injury of that sort, a physical therapist would stress the range of motion in order to break up the formation of scar tissue. This seemed like an interesting possibility. A hole in the forest floor had substituted for conventional medicine. Later that fall, I choreographed and danced in a piece based on teachings of the medicine wheel. My knee was fully functional. I had certainly learned some important lessons about how to work with trauma, but not exactly in the way I had originally imagined. I had set an intention to learn, and I had been carefully instructed.

2. What Is an Intention?

Setting an intention at the beginning of any endeavor significantly strengthens and guides the outcome. An intention differs from a goal. Achieving a goal is a linear, step-by-step process. There is a specific end in mind, and there are known steps that need to be taken in order to achieve this end. For example, if I want to become an acupuncturist, I know that I will have to meet the requirements to get into an acupuncture school, make application to the school, complete the training and internship requirements, take the certification exam, become licensed, and set up my practice. The path is laid out before me.

An intention is different. It is a framework for possibilities, happening within the circle of life. We set the stage by clearly asking to learn something. In this example, I may know that I want to change careers, but I do not have a clear idea of what I want to do. I could set a goal to find out what I am best suited for, take personality and interest tests, and complete a workbook on career change. Or I may decide that I would like to learn how I can best serve creation, given who I am and what I have to offer. I don't need to know how I am going to learn. I set the intention. Perhaps I will choose to do the tests and workbook, and I will also pay very close attention to the information and experiences that are put in my path. I need to be careful about what I am asking for, because I need to be ready to accept responsibility for the information that comes. In other words, am I really willing to let go of preconceived notions and be open to new possibilities?

---

8   The Good Medicine Society, in its modern form, is based on the teachings of Eli Gatoga, a Cherokee medicine man who, in 1971, had a vision that sacred spiritual teachings, which had previously been passed down only through certain families, should now be made available to anyone who would like to take the time to learn.

3. Creating an Intention

Having begun her journal, Sue came to her second psychotherapy session. She recognized that she was about to embark on an important journey. Because she was a person who had always worked hard to please everyone and to be perfect in every way, to start a journey without knowing where she was going was incredibly brave. Instead of carefully planning every step of the way and mapping it all out ahead of time the way she had always done before, she was going to take whatever road appealed to her at the moment, as she arrived at each fork. She was willing to experiment with a whole new way of doing things. This did not mean that the old way was bad. She was simply expanding her repertoire of ways of being and acting in the world.

Her old way was to do everything in a linear fashion. Goals were carefully set. The steps to achieve the goals were thoughtfully mapped out. And with determination and discipline, she would head down a known route to accomplish something that she had decided was important. There were other ways that she could have chosen to determine the direction of her healing journey. These would have been very unlike her too. She could have let the fates determine the outcome of her journey. Or she could have chosen to exercise her free will to decide to the best of her ability what she wanted to learn from the process that she was about to enter.

Sue and I did some talking about what she wanted. Later in her journal, she wrote down her thoughts. "I want to do what is necessary to let myself work toward complete wellness physically, emotionally, and spiritually." We simplified this further to, "I want to embrace complete wellness." This was her intention.

When another client named Jennifer began her therapy, she felt that her life was rather meaningless. Her parents never encouraged her to go to college. She had taken some classes and found out that what she thought she would like (engineering) was not for her. She felt like there was a deficit of information in her life. She wanted more. She wanted to understand her higher purpose, but she had no specific goal to work toward. This was a perfect opportunity for her to create an intention. There was no goal with specific steps to achieve it. There was a desire, a heartfelt desire, to discover a new career that was better suited to her talents. Because she had no specific focus, she needed to use an intention rather than a goal.

Jennifer began by writing down some of her ideas in her journal and by talking them over with me and a friend. She said, "I know that my life is empty right now. There has to be more to life than this, but I haven't a clue in which direction to head. I know more about what I don't want than what I do want. Life is about having something to give back once you have learned some skills. I know I am an intelligent person and that I have some special gifts. How do I make these gifts into a higher purpose? This higher purpose needs to serve not only myself, but also the larger community. I really want to understand my higher purpose in a way that I can begin pretty soon. My children are growing up and my intense mothering days will soon be over. Who am I . . . beyond mother? Who am I . . . beyond worker bee? How do I fit into the bigger picture? What do I have to offer?"

Starting with laying out some rambling thoughts, she then read them over and picked out a few key phrases. "I want to understand my higher purpose. I want to know who I am and what I have to offer the world. I want this offering to come from my desire to do service, really as I think of it, for the higher good of all created."

Now she was ready to word the specific intention. "My intention is to learn how I can best serve by living out my highest potential." That became a simple straightforward statement that included her beginning ideas.

In order to create an intention when you feel a strong desire for change, experiment with some words to describe your desire. You might write out a paragraph or two or talk over your ideas with a friend. This process of clarification helps you to create one open-ended sentence that states your intention in the positive.

As is often the case, Jennifer had some fears that she needed to face in order to make her intention clearly without hesitation. "What does it mean to serve? Will my life radically change? What about my children? What about my loved ones? What about my lifestyle? What about saving money for the future? What about having money for retirement?" These were some of the fears that came to the surface as she began to consider how letting go of her unpleasant yet secure future might play itself out. If she truly allowed herself to embrace her intention, what would be asked of her?

Facing fears is important. Sometimes, just the acknowledgment of them is enough to feel them dissipate. Sometimes there is more work to be done. By using a process discussed in the section of this book on the shifting and releasing of feelings, she was able to move through these feelings to love herself enough to embrace her heart's desire.

My experience is that we are never asked to do more than we can handle. As we embark on our journeys, we may be asked to take some very big steps that make us wobble a little. Remember that you are always free to say yes or no to any experience. I could have skipped the healing ceremony in the incident with my knee and gone straight to the doctor. God gave each of us the free will to choose, and God will never override our choices. In fact, he/she will do all within his/her power to support us in the choices we make, good ones and not so good ones.

One way to think about it is that our souls are birthed here on earth in order to gather information though these beautifully complex sensory instruments called bodies. We expand our soul's experience through a process of making mistakes, learning, and growing. Do you remember back to a time when you would study very hard for an exam? You did very well and missed only several of the questions. If you were being a good student, you would take the time to look up and correct the information that you had missed. Let's say that five years passed by, and for some reason, you needed to recall the information that had been covered on that test. Would you be more likely to remember the information from the questions that you got right or the ones you had missed but corrected? More than likely, you would remember the corrected information long after the other information had faded away. The lessons we learn from the mistakes we make often last us a lifetime.

When I injured my knee by jumping off a log four feet high onto one leg instead of two, I could have become very angry with myself for being so stupid. I knew better and should have jumped down onto both legs. I could have focused on my mistake and on my stupidity. I could have felt sorry for myself and been angry with God. "Why me?" I had a very different plan for my time at LaPush. I could have focused on all of the fun that I was missing, instead of the incredible lesson that was handed to me by the universe. If I had followed this path, I would have been swamped by great deal of negative energy and been miserable. Choosing to see this "mistake" as an opportunity to learn about how to deal with trauma opened me up a new level of awareness and helped me develop new patterns of response. I was taught not only how to do this for myself, but also how I might help others who suffer from other or similar traumatic events in their lives.

When the trauma occurred in my knee, there was a radical disruption to the existing energetic patterns holding my knee in healthy form. This energetic disruption spilled over into my emotional energy and into my mind. I experienced a feeling of panic and had thoughts of torn ligaments and displaced cartilage. The accompanying thought that this event was part of the learning I had set in motion with my intention helped me to shift into a response that was different for me. I knew that I had to focus on recreating energetic patterns of balance and harmony, health and wholeness, calmness and love. I began by praying and asking for help from the earth and the spirit guides that worked with me. Sending loving thoughts to my knee, I held it and I began to hum. I did not know to do this ahead of time. I learned the importance of repatterning disrupted energy fields. I experimented with several ways to do this through prayer, sound, visualization, Reiki, flower essences, and the use of stones and cedar. I can now offer my clients a conceptual framework for what happens when trauma occurs and encourage them to experiment with a variety of ways to repattern their energies.

4. Putting the Intention into Prayer

The next step is to put your intention in the context of a prayer. Sue's prayer went like this: "I do believe there is a God, a Creator. How can I see the color in the trees, the sky, the flowers and feel the warmth of the sun and the breeze on my face and hear the waves and not believe in God? How can I hear a fetal heartbeat (she was an OB-GYN nurse) and not believe in God? I certainly don't understand everything about God, but please, God, open my heart, hear my prayer, my plea for help. Show me what I need to do. Help me to see, to understand. Give me the courage I need, the wisdom to recognize what it is you want to tell me. I do believe in angels. If you can spare some help, please send it in my direction. Make me understand that I am not being selfish to want this. Because you have not always been a large part of my past, I hope that I'm not too late to ask for help, for guidance. I can't seem to find comfort in myself the way I am. Give me the strength to make positive changes, so I can find that comfort. Help me to like and respect myself. I want to embrace complete wellness. Amen"

Jennifer's prayer was, "Dear Lord God, I stand humbly before you. I am grateful for the beauty and wonder of all of life. It is my intention to learn how to best serve by living out my highest potential. I am asking you for help and guidance. I choose willingly to surrender and trust in the everlasting flow of love in the universe. Amen"

By stating your intention in the form of a prayer, you are aligning your will with your conscious intention. A clear and succinct energetic message is sent to God and the universe, and this message opens the door for a clear energetic response.

5. Creating an Altar

Since time
immemorial, the
primary function of
altars and shrines has
been to provide sacred
and holy places amid
the ordinary reality
of life[9]

Denise Linn

You may want to set up an altar in a special corner of your favorite room to honor the intention that you write out on a piece of paper. Put the written intention on the altar along with those objects that have special value to you. These may be a beautiful stone you found at the beach, a feather that lay in your path, a crystal given to you by a friend, a picture of someone who looks like she/he feels empowered to be her/his best, perhaps a candle, and a bowl of water all laid out on a cloth given to you by your grandmother.

---

[9]   Denise Linn, *Bringing Sacred Shrines into your Everyday Life: Altars* (New York: Ballantine Wellspring, 1999), p. 11.

There are many ways to create altars. It is constructed to suit you and your intention, for its purpose is to help you focus your attention, energy, and prayers on the intention that you are setting.

I have recently come to understand the importance of altars as part of the process of setting an intention. Two dear friends and I are in the process of trying to buy land adjacent to my property. This land is to be held in sacred trust with the earth. We are developing a community and will use the land for retreats, ceremonies, and workshops to educate others about how to live close to the earth and honor her with every step. We have set the intention for the land and placed an altar at the "belly button" of the property. It consists of a slice of an oak log that has a hole in the center. Members of the spiritual community who gather there each brought something to contribute: a special necklace, a shell, a favorite crystal, a beautiful stone. Faithfully, we had been going to the altar at the full moon to pray for the success of our venture. Sadly, the purchase of the land was moving along at an excruciatingly slow pace. For almost three months, we had an offer on the table, and we had heard nothing, even with a reminding phone call.

What were we to do? Were we supposed to push, or were we supposed to sit and patiently wait? Ellen, a member of the community, consulted with the Council of ADRON. This council is made up of spirits that define themselves as a group intelligence. The individuals in this group are ascended masters, angels, and star beings. My sister Starfeather participates with the council and is their spokesperson. They replied, "We understand that you have set up an altar at the center of the land. That is good. How often do you go there to pray?" At Ellen's reply, they responded, "Oh, at the full moon. Now let's see. That makes twelve prayers a year . . ." By this time, we were laughing and getting it. Gee, twelve prayers a year for something that felt very important. Okay, okay, we could up the ante and pray a lot more than that.

They also suggested that we place crystals that have been cleared and asked to hold the intention of the land around the perimeter of the property. That's a lot of crystals, and we have a whole community of people who were willing to help. The first Saturday that we met to plant the crystals, we made it about a third of the way around the property. Some bees stung my dog and Mike, who was trying to rescue the dog. Other bees stung another young man, Brian, as he ran to see if he could help. We decided that it was time to quit for the day, so we made our way back through the thick woods to my house.

One friend stayed to visit a little after the others had left. The phone rang. It was the owner of the property. We had a pleasant chat, and I was able to ask for permission to camp on the land. He had not forgotten us but had been tied up with other business. The increased prayers and crystals had begun their magic much more quickly than I had imagined. Perhaps the crystals were a way of expanding the energy of the altar. It felt as if this ring of light embraced the "belly button" as we pledged ourselves to the earth to hold her in sacred trust.

At a later date, when we were told that our offer was unacceptably low, we understood that we needed to pray for the family that held the land, especially the mother for whom the money was designated as retirement income. The Council of ADRON suggested that we were setting unnecessary financial limits by thinking that this was how much we could offer and no more. Why not believe in the truly abundant universe and ask to be provided with more money than she was asking? This was certainly a different attitude. I saw that I had been putting up a roadblock to abundant possibilities by being angry that she would ask for more money than the appraised value. Perhaps she had her own fears about being taken care of in her old age, and we were after all praying for the highest good to come for all concerned. Why not open up the floodgate of green energy to provide for all of what was necessary and more? To stubbornly limit the amount of money on principle (she shouldn't get more than what the land was worth), on righteous judgment (she was being greedy), or on having to make a good deal put a negative spin on the basic intention and contaminated the energy with which it is put out into the universe. Attaching negative energy to the intention will result in a negative outcome. Like attracts like. Perhaps the land deal was moving slowly so that we would have an opportunity to learn the many lessons being made available to us through this process.

Here are examples of other altars: My abundance altar has various symbols of abundance placed on it. There are Chinese coins; a pod full of seeds; a small brass box filled with pennies my mother collected; a "circle of friends" candle; a picture of my son, his wife, and newborn daughter; a small cluster of quartz crystals; a small Mexican papier-mâché house with a village of people in it; and a basket of beach treasures that I have collected over the years.

Another altar holds the intention of a loving relationship for the highest good. The backdrop is a beautiful red silk scarf embroidered with flowers given to me by my first husband Malcolm. There are two carved swans, birds that mate for life; a picture of Osiris and Isis, for eternal life; rose quartz, for good heart energy; a woven heart-shaped ceramic basket, which holds a very beautiful handmade soap; another crystal in which pyrite and tourmaline are intermixed; and two voluptuously flowering plants in painted red pots.

Another altar on the coffee table in the living room honors the sacred feminine. On the wall behind it is a large watercolor that I did of the earth as a woman: trees spring from her mountainous breasts, a river flow down her arm, etc. On the table, I have a large white porcelain statue of Kuan Yin seated on a large lotus flower. She is the Chinese goddess of mercy and compassion and is also the protectress of children. The lotus symbolizes purity, perfection, divine birth, and spiritual fruitfulness. The statue is placed on a pretty green Guatemalan placemat. Stones, spiral shells, and small crystals ring the base of the statue like a beautiful necklace of earthly treasures. A turtle shell, which represents the earth, is there, as well as a red candle and a ceramic vase in the shape of a female torso filled with fresh flowers. A cluster of quartz crystals sits in front of her and a philodendron sits beside her.

In my meditation room, I have an altar for the Naraya, a Native American dance that I attend several times a year. The dance takes place around the Tree of Life and has an intention to heal the earth. In order to bring healing to the greater whole, each dancer is asked to set an intention for personal healing. It is on this altar that I place my carefully crafted intentions in the center of a medicine wheel that is made of small stones. This dance honors the ancestors, so there is a picture of my mother, who is no longer living. I place my medicine bag, which carries a few secret treasures that are very meaningful to me personally and a turquoise necklace given to me by one of the bundle keepers. Sand, cedar, and tobacco collected from the dances I have attended, as well as a picture I drew of my hand holding the earth in my palm with spiraling light emanating from its center, decorate it.

Altars can be simple or complex. They are places of beauty whose theme reflects the intention it holds and serves as a reminder. Altars serve as a concrete reminder of the intention that has been set. They focus the energy of the prayers and meditations that happened around them, helping to make the process even more powerful.

6. Letting Go

Use the altar for up to twenty-one days or more if necessary to focus your attention on what you are asking to create. Do not focus your attention on how the intention might come to pass. The universe is good at handling the details without your help.

Many of my clients groan when I begin to talk to them about this step. To let go means to let go of all of the worries about how the intention is going to come to pass. Some people seem convinced that the more they analyze the information they have about a situation, the more likely they are going to force the resolution into being. Have you ever had the experience of not being able to come up with a piece of information you know very well, like someone's name, and the more you think about it, the more you can't remember it? It seems to hang just out of reach in the back of your mind. It is only when you decide to let it go and give up the worry about not remembering that name or whatever the information you were seeking that it pops back into your conscious awareness. The intention is much the same. You need to be aware of and energize what you are asking for through prayer and the altar.

Worry creates negative energy. Usually, we worry because we are afraid. If you are feeling fear around what might happen if your intention comes into being, then it is very important to pay attention to those fears as well as to identify and release them. Worry and fear send a negative message to the universe, which will respond in like kind. This is why care is taken to create the intention in the positive. "I intend to learn how to be comfortable in social situations," not "I intend to learn how not to feel inadequate and awkward in social settings."

7. Paying Attention

Your job is simply to pay attention. Heighten your conscious awareness of everything around you. A hawk may unexpectedly swoop in front of your car in a very uncharacteristic manner. You may have an unusually clear dream, which you take the time to write down. A book jumps off the shelf in the bookstore into your hand. Some long lost friend may call you on the phone and say something unexpected to you. This may all be related to your intention, some of it symbolic, some of it very straightforward.

A number of years ago, I was going through the very painful demise of a relationship. I had set the intention to heal the pain of betrayal and come to a place where I could love him unconditionally. For three days straight, I found snakes on my path. Once dancing down my driveway after a very affirming conversation on the phone with someone, a very long beautiful black snake lay partly across the road. He stayed still while I watched him.

The next day, a big black snake was in the woodpile at the sweat lodge. He scooted away as I drew the tarp back. The third day, I was hanging sweet grass, lavender, and oregano in the garage to dry, when my cat called my attention to a large copperhead curled up in the corner of the garage. I sat and watched him for a while. His tongue darted in and out, working to sense me. He seemed to be saying to me, "All of life lives in your circle, the harmless and the poisonous. Don't be naive or afraid. Pay attention to the lessons that each brings. Each has a valuable contribution to the whole. It is how you react that counts. Face the poison. Don't run away. Embrace it. If you bring it into you without fear, you will transform the energy into something positive."

With such an abundance of snakes one after the other, I decided to read what Jamie Sams had to say about snakes in her book on animal medicine. She speaks of snakes transmuting poisons and having powerful creative energy. Sexuality, psychic energy, alchemy, reproduction, and immortality are also aspects of snake's teaching. The snake sheds its skin in a life-death-rebirth cycle.

I was certainly deep in the middle of a cycle of death and rebirth. In this relationship, I had ignored the strong intuitive messages that something was wrong. I was too comfortable on some level to give up the relationship, so I chose to believe his lies instead. I needed to learn to embrace chaos. I had been so busy trying to keep us both afloat that I had failed to listen to my own intuitive voice. I had tried to control too much, more than what was mine to control. And I had enabled an unhealthy situation to continue. The snakes were reminding me that running away from chaos only brought more forward. Embracing the poison would allow the process of transmutation to occur. The cycles could then flow with ease. Rebirth could occur, and there would be a chance to begin again. I had set the intention to heal my old patterns of behavior, release emotional attachments, and move to a place of forgiveness and compassion for him and myself. The ending of this relationship brought many lessons that were initiating a new cycle of growth. The snakes had shown up to shed more light on the intention I had set.

8. Loving Yourself Enough

Loving yourself enough to manifest your heart's desires can be a joyful task. Remembering to slow down, relax, and stay in the present reminds you that all is unfolding exactly as it is meant to be. The setting of intentions is not a way to control the outcome, but a process of setting up a framework for possibilities. It is learning to trust and love in something beyond your ego. It is going slowly enough to pay attention and ask the universe for assistance.

Sometimes the outcomes will be dramatic and very noticeable, and at other times, the shifts in perception and energy will be subtle. Be careful what you ask for. When I set the intention to learn to heal trauma, I thought I was going to learn through the experience of my clients. The universe had something else in mind. I needed to be an active participant and learn through my own experience. Setting intentions paves the way for new learning and an opportunity to embrace internal changes.

Patty's story is an example of how a simple intention profoundly affected her life. Her husband was an officer in the military. He was a bright man who was making his way up the ranks. Patty's father had been a ranking officer in the army. She was used to the military way, which meant moving a lot and being the model wife and citizen. She and her husband both thought that she was well prepared to assist his climb to the top.

They shared a deep common spiritual core that gave them an agreed-upon, clear set of values. They chose to home-school their children, eat healthy organic foods, join the food co-op and be active in church. She participated as an officer's wife, doing what she needed to do to make her husband look good.

Her husband was gone more and more with school and work. His work days stretched from ten to twelve to fourteen hours, plus a long commute to and from work. Yes, he was advancing his career. She was very proud of his accomplishments, yet she was increasingly lonely. The burden of the house, the yard, the children, and their education fell more and more on her shoulders. She found that she was all by herself, holding up the core of values, which they had set for their family. The weight of it grew heavier as the children grew older and became involved in more activities. She loved being a mother, but the many masks she wore began to crack. Her face began to hurt along with her heart.

Gradually, she began to feel her own needs as a person. She was beginning to love herself enough to ask for more. Where was there room for her to discover who she was and what she had to offer? She joined a poetry writing group and began to discover that she had feelings separate from her husband's and separate from her father's. She had her own identity to explore.

Patty made a prayer. "God, in your deepest wisdom, help me discover the true me, so that I may serve you to the fullest. I desire to walk in my own truth." She was setting her intention.

This did not mean she wanted to divorce or to stop being a mother. She was very devoted to her children and her husband. Yet there needed to be room for her as well. There needed to be mutual respect. Her role as a homemaker needed to be seen as having value. Her thoughts and ideas needed to be a viable part of the decision-making process. She wanted to claim herself as a whole person, committed to a valuable partnership with her husband, herself, children, and God.

Within a few days after her prayer, she began to shake, literally shake all over. An earthquake had hit her being and was shaking it from the foundation. She felt intense anxiety, became deeply disturbed, and ended up in the hospital on the psych ward. "Nothing really happened in the hospital, but I sent all of the nurses roses after I left. They must have felt I was really crazy. After the hospital stay, we went for long walks and prayed together. Even though I was scared, I was really happy. My husband's focus shifted. My own focus got clearer. He tried to listen to what I was feeling. I was beginning to feel me." Her powerful intention in the form of a prayer initiated a journey into wholeness.

The spiraling road continues to wind its way upward, as Patty discovers the incredible jewels within her and also works to keep her relationship with her husband growing. The setting of the intention in the form of a prayer had a very powerful effect. It was scary at first, and then it became more and more joyous as she became clearer about what she needed to learn.

Another time, when I was facilitating a women's therapy group, I asked the women to set an intention for the ten weeks that they would be together. One of the women said that she intended to heal past hurts that had resulted from betrayals in relationships with others. She felt as if there was a pattern in her life that she was ready to resolve. It was very interesting to watch how the universe arranged the details for her. Part of the group agenda was to learn about various forms of alternative healing. Unbeknownst to me, one of the healers I invited to teach the group was a childhood friend of this woman. She had felt betrayed by this woman when they were much younger. Outside of our group meeting, she ran into a man who had been a past lover. She had not seen this man in years. She took both of these opportunities to work on letting go of old hurts.

Inspired by the healing group she had worked with for over a year and by a print of beautiful women resting after a temple ceremony that hung in the ladies room at Breitenbush (a beautiful hot springs retreat center in the Cascade Mountains in Oregon), my sister Starfeather decided she would like to create a healing temple. This would be a place where people could come to take the time to find out who they were and learn to embrace the beauty of their bodies, minds, and spirits. She had no money, no land or building to begin such a venture, so she decided to set an intention, put her prayers out into the universe, create an altar, and see if she could manifest the healing temple.

She had been talking about the healing temple since our January trip to Breitenbush. The more she thought about it, the clearer the image became in her mind, and the more passionate she felt. On her annual spring equinox shield-building retreat, she decided to put these ideas down in the form of a shield, a cedar branch woven into a circle. She stretched leather across the branch and glued some stones around the bottom half to represent the spiritual ancestors who were keeping the temple in a sacred manner. She fashioned a small ladder out of twigs to remind her that creating the temple was a step-by-step process. A crystal was placed above the golden symbol of the temple in order to focus energy on her intention and her prayer to the Creator.

During the course of her second workshop, at midweek, she decided to make that shield into an altar by suspending it from some pieces of driftwood. She placed stones, a candle, and other power objects around it. She took the time to sit quietly with it, to pray and meditate about her center. By the end of the workshop, one of the participants told her that she had twenty beautiful acres of pristine woods at the edge of a mountain river. She had always dreamed that the place would be a healing center of some sort, and now she would like to offer that land to Starfeather for her work.

My sister thanked her very much, not knowing quite what else to do. She could hardly believe it was really true. It was one thing to pray a powerful prayer one day, but then to have the very thing she had been praying for fall directly into her lap the next is quite another. This was a bit overwhelming. When she had made the ladder representing the step-by-step process, she had envisioned a ten-year plan to accomplish it. Instead, the offer of the land came within a week of creating the intention and altar.

The universe has its own timetable.

Later, she discovered that there was an additional thirty acres for sale adjacent to the woman's land. These acres would help give even more room for her ideas. And then there was the building of the temple. How would she ever find enough money? She continued to pray and talk about her vision with friends and others she met. A friend told her that she was a good friend with a woman who had inherited a great deal of money through very tragic circumstances. The woman wanted this money go to projects that would help heal the planet. Maybe this would be the source of the necessary funds to buy the additional land and build the healing temple.

The healing temple was to be an expression of the earth with the old woods, the moss, the river, and the stones being as integral a part of the temple as the building that would house baths and rooms. It was to be a place of beauty where people came and experienced their sacredness. By stepping out of ordinary reality, they would have the opportunity to discover their inner as well as their outer beauty. They would be given beautifully colored robes, fed wholesome food, and be well taken care of. Each one would be guided on his or her own personal journey to experience the Sacred Feminine.

It was a very beautiful vision, whose ongoing trail of manifestation holds interesting lessons for all of us. Several years later, my sister wrote this:

> Dear Friends of the Sacred Earth Healing Temple,
>
> I want to share with you where I am on this long journey. If you are receiving this letter, you have been good enough to walk with me down this pathway. I appreciate your advice and counsel, your love and support. We all want to do our best to follow our dreams, and I have not one regret. I have learned many things along the way and now feel it is time to acknowledge the closing of this chapter and the beginning of something new.
>
> Somewhere in the mid-'90s, I had a spirit vision of the Sacred Earth Healing Temple. It felt like a calling from Spirit to create again the great temples of old, in honor of the art of healing. To bring healers together, not to work as competitors, but as a team of co-creators with Spirit and with the earth, for people, who would perhaps come great distances, to stay and be renewed. The image was of a place very grand, with walkways in nature, fountains, rose quartz floor in a circle cathedral-like space. The vision was so large, beyond the beyond, it seemed unobtainable: only a miracle could make it happen.
>
> Lesson 1:   Miracles happen. I was offered the use of a beautiful piece of land on which to build a temple. I considered this offer over a two-year period, until it became apparent that the landowner and I had some different ideas, which made working together difficult. I had to walk away from this generous offer and hold the vision.
>
> Lesson 2:   If you build it, it should be on land you own and control, and everyone involved needs to be in full alignment with the vision. Good communication skills are a must. Many people have similar dreams and still are not meant to work together. Each dream is valid.
>
> I was then offered a house at half its listed value, in my lovely hometown that was on an acre of land. This came to me because I had written to a newspaper about my dismay that so many trees were being cut down. I had dedicated my year of 1999 to tree awareness. The owner did not want her property to go to a developer, who would do just that, cut down every tree.

Lesson 3:   Even when the gift is generous, if it's not right, it's not right, and you have to say no. The property just wasn't right for our needs, and with the help of a council of friends and the reality that even at half price, it was too pricey for me as an individual, I had the right to say, 'No, nice try, Spirit, but no.' I was not willing to go into deep personal financial debt.

Lesson 4:   Perhaps this project of creating the temple was more than putting up a yurt somewhere and more than I could personally handle. Perhaps if I created a nonprofit organization, I would be able to receive donations.

Lesson 5:   Be careful what you ask for. I felt very guided to an amazing property in Duvall, a lovely home on sixteen acres of land with gardens, ponds, and woods. The possibilities were endless of how this land could be used to create a temple worthy of the vision. It felt very expansive. The next task was to find the people who felt called to help finance it and set up a way for them to do that.

Lesson 6:   Creating a 501(c)3 is not a simple task and requires particular skills. I did not have those skills and had to find people who could do that type of work as volunteers. I was blessed to have a number of people step forward to offer help. My task was to find the other person(s) with financial abundance. I took at least sixty people out to that land in the next nine months and had a few long-distance potential connections, but the right person never showed up. Nothing clicked.

Lesson 7:   Sacred timing. I started showing this land to people in May of 2001. September 11, 2001, changed everything. It took quite a while to feel the ripple effect of that event. My investor/donator of funds evaporated. I finally realized in March 2002 that things were different. I felt I had done all that was asked of me by Spirit and to continue the search was a waste of my time. At first I had a sense of failure, but then I realized that no, things had changed. I needed to change too.

Lesson 8:   I felt that one reason it hadn't worked was that I was not honoring the spiritual foundation of the temple that it was, in fact, a church. I went as far as registering SEHT as a church in the state of Washington and received the paperwork for doing so from the federal government. It is another form of 501(c)3 . . . and the

paperwork made my head spin. I came close to hiring
someone to do it, but it just didn't feel right.

Lesson 9: Go with the flow. Go where there is "juice." I had to be
willing to let go of how I thought this was all going to
work and release the vision. It was freeing to do so. I
pulled the vision back home into myself.

Lesson 10: Who am I? And what do I *really* REALLY want? What if I
am the temple? I realized that what I wanted more than
anything else was to be a healer. (Not a wellness-center
director, and not a landscaper or event coordinator.) I
have worked as a healer in several different ways: doing
my energy drawings and doing readings through
facilitating retreats and circles, doing journey work,
ceremony, even some hands-on healing, and just being
with people. Still, I felt reluctant to say that I am a healer.

Lesson 11: Ask, and when the timing is right, you shall receive. I
asked on several occasions—in ceremony, in prayer,
and in my dreams—to be shown my true path. I asked
to be a healer in such a way that I could work on a global
scale. I left space in my schedule, changing my routine,
and opening the door to new possibilities by letting go
of some commitments that were becoming not quite so
juicy. And almost instantly, those empty spaces were
filled with the amazingly strong call to learn a new
healing modality that seems in perfect alignment my
gifts. Reconnective Healing and The Reconnection™
training was held during the times I had left open on
my schedule.

Lesson 12: When the right thing shows up, you know. I am feeling
so affirmed and thankful that I have no doubts about
my work as a healer now. Every other part of my life is
shifting and adjusting. And I am filled with *joy!* JOY It
takes no courage to make these changes because I am
so in alignment with my soul's purpose that there is no
struggle. It's fun.

Lesson 13: Gratitude. I am so filled with gratitude for everyone
who is supporting me in this transition: my husband,
my sister, my friends, my gallery team, and the business
itself. I have a space in my home where I can work in
beauty and comfort. I don't have to build a thing! I have
come to realize that many people trust me, which is
perhaps one reason why I may have been given this job

to do. I am worthy of it and can do it well. I feel like I have been doing it forever. And it too will change and evolve.

Lesson 14: It's not over. I am still holding the vision of the temple in my heart. For now, it is my new business called the Sacred Earth Center for Healing. I picture a huge V. At the top of the V is the temple of my vision, with those rose quartz floors. I was attempting to ground that vision in a way that did not work. I think it does exist, just not here, not now. I am at the point of the V, and I am expanding upwards. Perhaps the day will come when the temple and the healers are together again.

Thanks for giving me the time to explain.

My love and blessings,
Starfeather

Now she is using the Sacred Earth Healing Temple as a place where she takes people when she is doing healing work for them. It is not an actual place in physical form but in energetic form. She invites her clients to come with her to this place and describes it in detail to allow them to experience it as well. They work together in this sacred space and their work is augmented by the energetic reality of the temple. She is having a lot of fun with this new way of being and feels the power of it manifesting in healing.

This dream, which had been set as an intention through a process of clarification and put down in the form of a shield, became the focus of her prayers. The shield became an altar created to honor the temple. The dream is working its way into expanded possibilities, not by any preset formula but by synchronistic events that seemed to flow out of nowhere. As you can see, there are many powerful lessons being offered as a powerful dream unfolds and transforms.

The process of setting the intention is important. Wording it carefully, saying prayers, and creating an altar are ways to bring good energy to the project or desire. I used to think that letting the intention go meant letting it go completely. Now I understand that letting go means letting go of all of the worries about how the intention will come to pass. It is best to bring good, positive energy to the intention. Worrying about the intention is liable to create negativity. The quality of energy surrounding the intention sends a message to the universe about what is being asked for and draws to it like a magnet a similar energetic pattern. A weak desire or confused energy will call a long slow response, if any. A worrisome energy is likely to call the opposite of what you really want. Good, strong, passionate, clear energy calls a good, strong, passionate, clear response.

An intention can be set for a project, a ceremony, a circle, or a meeting. The intention I set for this book is that "in co-creative partnership, I want to teach how to live life from the heart in a holy and sacred way that is easily understood and applicable to modern life."

Not too long ago, some guidance was given to me that I needed to set an intention for the rest of my life. The task felt overwhelming because the time frame was potentially so long. How would I set up a framework for possibilities that could encompass so many years? How could I know what it was that I wanted to learn well into the future? How could I set something up that was open ended and creative enough to move with the tides of my life's journey? I began to realize that I was going to be making a statement about my deepest beliefs and values that would serve as a guiding light in the years to come. I chose to spend the night in the Sweat Lodge in order to talk it out through prayer and seek guidance from the spirits who work with me. After a night of contemplation, my statement became clear, "I intend to live my life as a loving, conscious, intentional, active, co-creative partner with *all there is* in the present moment for the highest good of all of life."

According to Eli Gatoga, the founder of the Good Medicine Society, we are entering a time when we are being asked to know through our own experience. When Moses brought the laws down from the mountain, people were being asked to learn to obey laws that helped to establish a moral code and organize society. When Christ, Buddha, and Mohammed taught us the truth as they understood it, humans were learning how to have faith and believe in the truths according to others. At this time in the history of human spiritual development, Eli taught that we are no longer content to obey or believe the truths of others. We are compelled to know the truth as it emerges out of our own experience.

9. I Create My Day

The following is an excerpt from an interview with scientist Dr. Joe Dispenza in the movie *What the #$BLEEP*! Do We Know!?*

"I wake up in the morning, and I consciously create my day the way I want it to happen. Now, sometimes, because my mind is examining all the things that I need to get done, it takes me a little bit to settle down and get to the point of where I'm actually intentionally creating my day. But here's the thing.

"When I create my day and, out of nowhere, little things happen that are so unexplainable, I know that they are the process or the result of my creation. And the more I do that, the more I build a neural net in my brain that I accept that that's possible. It gives me the power and the incentive to do it the next day.

"So, if we're consciously designing our destiny—if we're consciously, from a spiritual standpoint, throwing in the idea that our thoughts can affect our reality or affect our life because reality equals life, then I have this little pact that I have when I create my day. I say, I'm taking this time to create my day, and I'm infecting the quantum field. Now, if it is, in fact, the observers watching me the whole time that I'm doing this and there is a spiritual aspect to myself, then show me a sign today that you paid attention to any one of these things that I created and bring them in a way that I won't expect. So I'm as surprised at my ability to be able to experience these things and make it, so that I have no doubt that it is coming from you.

"And so, I live my life in a sense, all day long, thinking about being a genius or thinking about being the glory and the power of God or thinking about being unconditional love. I'll use living as a genius, for example. And as I do that, during parts of the day, I'll have thoughts that are so amazing, that cause a chill in my physical body that have come from nowhere. But then, I remember that that thought has an associated energy. That has produced an effect in my physical body. Now that's a subjective experience, but the truth is that I don't think that unless I was creating my day to have unlimited thought, that that thought would come."

10. Dream Your Dream

This story, like the other stories in this book, demonstrates that we each have the power to create something really incredible. By loving yourself, you can use your intention as a new way to learn, as an important gift given on the road to discover who you are, to develop your relationship with the Divine, and, ultimately, to become one with all that is.

Setting an intention in the process discussed here is not about "the road to hell is paved with good intentions." Using this process is not a casual affair. The purpose of this process is to bring your body and mind in alignment with your spirit and with your higher self. Your higher self is an aspect of your soul and serves as the template for your journey into wholeness and sacredness.

Here is a list of possible intentions. Have fun experimenting with creating your own. Let these examples jump-start your heart's desire to learn to live a fuller, richer life through the use of setting intentions.

"I intend to love myself as much as I love other people."
"I intend to love others as much as I love myself."
"I intend to learn how to accept others for who they are."
"I intend to stop and notice the beauty in my life today."
"I intend to be fully present to my parents (friends, children, and partner)."
"I intend to learn how to accept and love my body."
"I intend to learn how to find healthy balance between work and play."
"I intend to learn to honor my body and mind by paying attention to what I put into me."
"I intend to be alive and healthy."

After the intention has been set, the prayer made, the altar created, pay attention to what the universe sends your way. It could happen quickly like it did for Patty and my sister with her healing temple, or it could happen more slowly, as it was with the purchase of our land. In the case of our land, there were some steps we needed to take first to become clearer before the purchase would happen. This was a learning process that took some time. We had reorganized our thoughts on ownership, and we needed to send prayers of love and support to the family who owns the land as we shifted out of our limiting beliefs about what was right. That would not have happened if the land deal had been finalized earlier. Sometimes, there may be good reasons for the slowness of events. Love yourself enough to dream your biggest dream and bring your heart's desire into reality.

1.   Recognize that loving yourself in a simple, non-egotistical way is very important.
2.   Set an intention to learn to love yourself.
3.   Be in touch with your feelings, all of them. Remember what it feels like to be loved by another. Experience those feelings in your body right now.
4.   Make room within for love by making peace with your imperfect self.
5.   Practice forgiving yourself and others.
6.   Recognize the beauty that is around you and in you every moment of every day.
7.   Touch the Divine within, breathe that place alive, and feel filled with the grace of God.
8.   Practice giving and receiving love a lot, equally with yourself, with others, and with all forms of life.

When you choose to use your free will to create an intention for learning, you send a signal to the universe. Love yourself enough to put the wheels in motion and to take a journey on the road of conscious learning and healing. The universe responds lovingly by providing the lessons you need and the healing you have asked for.

11. Steps for Setting an Intention

1.   *Create an intention* when you are ready to set up a framework for the possibility to learn something new: a new way to respond, new patterns of behavior, a healing journey, a project, a ceremony, a gathering or a class. Write a paragraph or two about your ideas, or talk them over with a friend to clarify your idea. Simplify by pulling out the most important parts into three or four sentences. Now write one sentence in the positive that powerfully states your intention.
2.   Put it into the *form* of *a prayer*, keeping it simple and clear.

3. *Set up an altar* by putting your written intention, meaningful objects, a candle, and a stone in a special private place. Take the time to come to your altar every day for up to three weeks in order to focus your attention on your intention. This gives it good energy.

4. *Let it go* in the sense that you do not need to worry about or know how the intention is going to come about.

5. *Pay attention* to what's happening to you in the present moment in order to learn the lessons that are being presented to you.

6. *Love yourself enough* to allow yourself to reach for your heart's desire and to learn the necessary lessons on the way.

CHAPTER II

Opening to the Divine Within

The Lord is in me, and the Lord is in you,
As life is hidden in every seed.
So rubble your pride my friend,
And look for Him within you.

When I sit in the Heart of His world
A million suns blaze with light,
A burning blue sea spreads across the sky,
Life's turmoil falls quiet,
All the stains of suffering wash away.

Listen to the unstuck bells and drums!
Love is here; plunge into its rapture!
Rains pour down without water,
Rivers are streams of light.
How could I ever express
How blessed I feel
To revel in such vast ecstasy
In my own body?

This is the music
Of soul and soul meeting,
Of the forgetting of all grief.
This is the music
That transcends all coming and going.

Kabir[10]

---

[10]   Kabir, translation by Rabindranath Tagore, assisted by Evelyn Underhill, *One Hundred Poems of Kabir* (London: India Society, Cheswick Press, 1914), pp. 64-65.

1. A Process for Getting Out of Our Own Way

Often, in order to live life in a sacred manner, we need to learn how to get out of our own way so that we can create the daily prayer that is living in each one of us. This is a process of learning to truly love ourselves so that we can also love others and all aspects of life. As we become loving beings, we give love, receive the love directed back to us and give love away again. We come to understand that there is an endless bounty of love available wherever and whenever we need it. We learn to open ourselves up to the boundless flow of *divine love*. It is available to you, to me, to your own worst enemy, to every living being. Love, whose source is the Divine One, does not pick and choose one over the other.

Come along with me as I go on an imaginary journey into a large cave deep within the belly of the earth.

Flashlight in hand, I walk down the sharp leaf-covered ravine in the forest to a low dark opening. Moist, cool air greets my face as I get down onto all fours. Dampness penetrates my jeans, bringing a sudden sensation of cold wetness to my knees and hands. I have to admit that even though I know deep inside that this is a safe place, I stop and take a few deep breaths to raise my courage and send a prayer to God, the earth, and the angel of protection, "Come walk with me. Keep me safe. It is my intention to enter this cave in a sacred manner. I ask permission to enter in order to open myself to the loving presence of the Divine."

Now, I feel ready, having set my intention, and prepare to crawl through the narrow opening. Shining the light ahead, I can barely make out a long tunnel slanting steeply downward. Pictures of snakes and spirals are carved into the narrow walls. They mark similar descents made by ancestors who have come to this sacred place long before me. The dank, earthy smell is pleasantly comforting. The tunnel widens slightly, taking a curve first to the right then to the left. Like a snake, twisting and turning, I crawl down into the belly of the Mother.

Ahead, there is a beautiful, luminous blue light reflecting off of the tunnel wall. I turn off the flashlight to get a better sense of it. As I move slowly in that direction, the light gets slightly stronger. Turning the last corner, a large lighted room opens out before me.

Apparently, a small shaft of sunlight has found its way through the treetops to the forest floor into the earth and down through the hole in the high-vaulted ceiling of the cave. I rest, poised on the small ledge at the edge of an almost perfectly round room. Illuminated dark stone walls are occasionally decorated by standing or seated figures, animals and curious symbols painted in red ochre. It is so beautiful and peaceful, as holy a space as any of the great French Gothic cathedrals. I climb down off the ledge and come to the center, stretching my aching limbs.

As I take long deep breaths, the moist, cool air moves comfortably in and out of my body. My feet, resting on the smooth stone floor, sense the subtle pulsating vibrations of the earth's heartbeat. As I pay more attention to these vibrations, they seem to fill my whole body with energy, until I, too, am pulsating with the rhythm of the heart of the earth. Every cell in my body is acting like a little drum, responding in sympathetic harmony.

My awareness shifts back to the energy coming from under my feet. I imagine long taproots, extending from the soles of my feet into the earth. As I breathe, I feel the energy flowing from deep within the earth up through the taproots into the soles of my feet, up through my legs, through hip joints into pelvis, vertebrae by vertebrae, up the spine and into my heart. There is a growing warmth in my belly, as if I am drawing up the fire from the center of the earth first into my belly and then into my heart. This warmth fills me with the deep sense of well-being. I feel that I am being held like a child, nurtured and loved unconditionally. It is as if every cell in my body and every nook and cranny in my mind is being cared for, accepted, and loved.

My heart feels warm and full.

The continuous rhythmic sound of my breath is amplified by the stone walls.

Slowly, I become aware of the sound of water dripping from the vaulted ceiling above and flowing from a slow spring at the far end of the cave floor. The water makes its way around smooth stones, collecting in a deep pool and flowing out through a small split in the back wall. As I open my awareness to the water, I feel it flowing in and around and through the cells in my body that begin to feel like the polished stones in the stream. The water washes through my body, and all of the unneeded memories and old patterns of unwanted behaviors float away with the water through the crack in the stone. I am becoming clean and new again.

Joyfully, the quiet peacefulness of my breath passes in and out of my body like the eternal rhythm of the earth's heartbeat. The quiet expansion and contraction that comes with each breath feels like the ebb and flow of the tides of the great vast oceans of the world.

As all of the chatter in my mind seeps away, there is nothing left but the sound of breath, water, and heartbeat.

I am free, empty, warm, and full.

Before long, I become aware of another kind of warmth at the top of my head. The shaft of light touches my crown, sending strength and the beauty of the sun. The more I pay attention to the top of my head, the warmer and more alive I feel. Continuing to breathe deeply, the energy of the sun moves into my body, bringing with it a sense of direction and power. This radiant energy feeds me very differently from that of the earth.

I take time to sense the difference.

The fire from above moves through the top of my head to the atlas and axis vertebrae that balance my skull. The liquid light continues to flow down through each vertebra in my neck and upper chest into my heart. Feeling the warmth and brilliance of this pathway, my heart becomes illuminated by the sun.

As the fire from above joins the fire from below, a strong love begins to flower in my heart. With every breath, this love floods my body and my mind until I feel holy and sacred from within. All fears of not being enough, not being good enough, not being worthy, or of being too much find no room in my heart.

Focusing on this love, I begin to trust in its reality and feel it fill my entire being, eradicating all artificial boundaries previously held between body, heart, and mind. Just as the spring fills the pool in the cave continually, so this love fills me. And like the pool in the cave, I experience the overflow. There is more than enough love: enough for me, for the earth, for the mountain top, for the valley below, for the sun above, for all my human and nonhuman friends and relatives, and even enough for my enemies. I am all of life, and the love that pours out of me is constantly being replenished by the love flowing into me from the earth and the sun, until there in no longer a me or an other.

We become one and the same . . .

When my awareness returns to the stone walls of the cave, the light has grown dim. In slow motion, I make my way back to the ledge, pick up the flashlight, and crawl on all fours up the winding tunnel.

Emerging from the earth feels like coming out of the birth canal, born anew.

Standing once again at the bottom of the ravine and feeling my feet on the earth, I look high above at the sliver of new moon and first stars that greet the cool, crisp night.

Still pulsating with the flow of *divine love*, I pause to thank the angel of protection, the earth, and God for this intensely beautiful experience. I ask, "When I become distracted and lose focus and my conscious awareness of the flow ceases, help me to remember to stop, to focus, to take the time to breathe deeply, and to remember this time. Help me to remember that *divine love* is always present, whether I am conscious of it or not. Help me to discover that the more I practice, the more consciously aware I will be of the continuous flow of energy and love in my entire being. Help me to remember to draw the *divine light* into myself and allow it to flow out to those around me, into the community and beyond, in an endless cycle of *divine love*. Thank you for this beautiful connection to the vibrant nature of all of creation."

Beech Trees in Winter Rain

Tiny beech fingers reach skyward
praying,
receiving,
gifts from the great Gray Cloud Nations.

Elephant skinned trunks stand
supporting,
conducting,
rivers of water from the branches above.

The beautiful Earth Mother holds
loving,
nourishing,
thick roots nestled deep within her body.

Under elephant skin the sap moves
slipping,
shipping,
abundant life force upward.
Singing,
the trees seem to say,
"I am a conduit of the loving energy between
God the Father and God the Mother."

2. Being in Divine Flow

During one of Dr. Rudy Bauer's Wednesday-morning seminars, there were a group of about fifteen people seated on multicolored pillows in an oblong circle. We began in the usual manner, entering the *field*[11] by centering our breathing, focusing inward first by extending our awareness downward and then upward. After the vertical was established, we connected with our ancestors behind and in front with the generations to come.

This reminded me about a powerful lesson I had while attending the Naraya, a Native American sacred dance, about our connection to our ancestors. I participated in a Sweat Lodge ceremony prior to the beginning of the dance and brought a newly acquired Lemurian quartz crystal to set on the altar. After being granted permission to place it there, wrapped in cedar and red cloth, I was asked if I had permission to do healing work with crystals. Since no one ever

---

[11]   The *field*, also called the primordial field of awareness, is the divine energy that pervades all space and all living things.

said to me directly that I had such permission, I hesitated. The Paiute medicine man then asked if I was willing to work with the crystal if it came alive in the lodge. There was no hesitation. I quickly responded, "Yes."

The powerful ceremony came and went, and I was never called on to work with the crystal. Because the ceremony had run on for a long time, we were late for lunch and the beginning ritual of preparation for the dance. I hurried to get my shower and change for the afternoon. In the middle of my shower, my heart sank. I had left the crystal on the altar, which was a very irresponsible thing to do. I ran back there as quickly as I could, but the crystal was gone. At lunch, I spoke to Marshal Jack, the Sweat Lodge leader. Yes, he had the crystal, but he was not going to give it back to me yet. There was a lesson to be learned.

While I was relieved that the crystal was safe, I knew that he had a right to keep it. Later in the day, I asked if I could have it to put on the altar under the Tree of Life in the center of our dance circle. He said, "No, it is not time yet." He wanted to talk to me.

Three days later, before breakfast, when our dance was complete and we were preparing for the closing ritual, I brought him a pouch of tobacco. As we sat over steaming coffee in the high desert mountains of Utah, he talked for a long time. He had taken time with the crystal and had seen its role in my life. This he did not share with me. However, one of the most powerful things he did say to me that morning was, "That crystal is very powerful medicine, and it has come to you because your ancestors have prayed for you. You are the answer to their prayers." Immediately, I understood in a new way the prayers of thanks for the teachers and seven generations that have gone before us and the prayers for the next seven generations.

This new meaning lent power to the connection we make with our ancestors in the opening of our work at Rudy's. They love us, hope for us, support us, even if we never actually knew them, because we carry their dreams, as well as our own, into the future.

As we entered into the *field* with conscious awareness that morning, we also took the time to connect with the holy people whom we have known, with the morphogenic fields of those spiritual practices that we embrace and with the White Brotherhood.[12] It is from this place within the *field* that we were listening to a talk that Rudy was giving on embodying primordial field of awareness.

On this particular day, I was having a hard time focusing on his words. He mentioned at one point about connecting the eyes with the heart. This is a concept that I had been practicing and was consciously trying to do it that morning, albeit with some effort. Later, the fellow who was sitting across the circle from me said that he could feel my energy strongly during the time I was using him as a focal point. Luckily, he was a good friend and didn't mind my

---

[12]   The White Brotherhood are advanced spiritual intelligence, "Light Beings" that have the responsibility of administering the Cosmic Law of YHWH. This definition is adapted from *The Keys of Enoch* by J.J. Hurtak, p569.

intrusion. I had no idea that I would be felt so strongly. It was important information.

Rudy also gave us a new breathing technique that consisted of a series of quick diaphragmatic in-breaths and a silent out-breath of "ahh" spoken from the heart with the mouth slightly open. Very quickly, that deepened my experience. I began to focus better and saw a lot of moving light and color. He then asked me to "stretch" people. The purpose of the stretching is to gently use touch on the shoulders, forehead, or heart to help the participant to open more deeply to their experience of the *field*. I was surprised that he asked me to do this activity this morning because I was struggling so to be fully present.

As I stood up and began to move toward the first person to my left, I became acutely aware of her energy field. I seemed to be engaged in it with my whole body and energy. I felt as if I knew exactly where and with what kind of pressure she needed to be stretched. Sometimes it was not even a matter of touching but engaging her energy with mine and pulling it open with my hands.

As I continued around the circle, my whole being became more and more attuned to the resonance of the *field*. At first, there was a Sufi chant playing, so there was external sound, as well as toning that came from within me. There was breath and undulating movements, sometimes loud and fast, sometimes hardly perceptible. There was so much love. I felt as if I was imbued with the presence of the divine and flowed in a current of *divine energy*. My body, of which I was fully aware, moved of its own accord. I was in a divine dance, swimming in a sea of resonant energy of light and love. While I was fully aware of my surroundings, my body, my breath, the heart-to-eye connection, it all flowed completely effortlessly. My focus had become singular and global at the same time.

As I moved from person to person, I could feel my focus shift pulling away from one and called into engagement with another. Each individual had a unique field with its own currents and eddies and needs. Every molecule in my being was responding to every molecule of their beings. Sometimes it was a matter of embracing with the energy of love (not physically touching) their field, sometimes it was pulling energetically at the heart chakra, sometimes it was stretching someone upward to a standing position and meeting them front to front with the whole of my energy. The dance was in me, and I was the dance of energy and light.

At one point, I engaged with Jan in our group. Our outstretched hands met, and I felt called to place my crown chakra on hers. (I was standing in front of her, and she was seated.) Energetically, this was enormously powerful: my whole being felt electrified. After I disengaged from her field, I had to take a moment to be sure that my feet were on the ground and to steady my energy before moving to the next person.

At the end of our seminar, Marilyn described her experience. As I had moved down to that end of the room, she felt the whole space become charged with energy. She saw me as a column of golden particles of light. On my part I felt other and myself simultaneously, as if I was moving and being moved in an intense sea of *divine energy* that resonated in and through each one of us in a unique way and was a whole much greater than all of us put together. Our being was filled with an immensity of love and beauty. I only knew that I wanted to keep dancing and relating in this manner for a very long time.

3. New York Naraya

The Naraya is an ancient Native American Dance of Shoshone and Paiute origin that celebrates our connection to all of life and our ability to manifest that connection through personal vision. Our experience of this rainbow community is strengthened as we come together to dance around the Tree of Life for the explicit intentions of honoring Mother Earth and supporting the personal intentions that each dancer brings to the dance. I have participated in this ritual a number of times and find it very powerful. This poem speaks about one experience I had when I had set the intention to become one with the Divine. It is an example of how both the eagle spirit and the spirit of the earth showed up to help.

Part I
Eagle spirit grabs me
shaking me out of my skin.

Stretching,
soaring,
reaching,
opening,
deep into starlit galaxies
plunging upward
we fly
engulfed by primordial bliss.
Love knows no bounds.
Despite urging,
I do not want to come home.

Suddenly,
recognizing this place:
Undulating blue sparks
of primordial life arranged
spaciously
Heavenly
lovingly
are deep in my Heart.

I am
Home with the Divine One
Always.

Part II
Skipping,
laughing,
playfully touching
the earth with my feet
My soul spills out
Everywhere.

4. The Council of ADRON

This was guidance I was given by the Council of ADRON that feels like it is for all of us. "There is the beautiful expression: 'Home is where your heart is,' and we would ask you to see and feel where your heart is. You are at once HOME and not at home. Again we give you a nonanswer to this question because there is NO HOME and everywhere is HOME. Be at peace, dear one. Open yourself up to the new reality and feel the LOVE that is truly all around you. The search, in a sense, is over. You will expand into this understanding over time. Be gentle with yourself and know you are where you are needed. Try to pace yourself so that you have time to step back and then time to be on high. Your greatest asset is your VOICE and your love expressed on the earth plane. Let your inspiration and passion guide you and be aware of the flow."

Now I experience that I am a river of light. Undulating forms of *divine light* move through the cathedral of my expanded physical form. Each molecule of my body has spread out to give more room for the divine expression in purples and blues and whites and pinks. The sweetness of this experience spreads ever outward. A smile creeps over my face. My fingers move in and out of ancient positions of recognition. Yes, I am remembering the ways of my spirit long ago when I was a river of light flowing.

I feed on the light that is my body and know no hunger. The long proboscus of my being dips into the honey pot of the divine flower, which, at the same time, reaches up to greet me, and we exchange essences. I once was a vampire, hungry for sexual experience to feed my passionate desire. Now I am a fruit bat riding the currents of holy light, opening my being in complete surrender to the juice of the universe.

It is my intention to be an expression of divine will on earth.

5. Opening to the Divine Within

1. Tonight, when you go to bed, take your own journey into the belly of the earth and discover what lies within for you.
2. Make a meditation tape for yourself by using your favorite relaxing music as background. Read the journey into the cave as a script.

3. Begin by speaking kindly to yourself and taking care of yourself as well as you would a new lover or your most beloved child.

4. Take the time to stop periodically during the day and tune into the earth and feel the warmth of the sun and the brightness of the stars and moon. Gather those energies into your heart. Move forward into the day from that place in the heart.

5. Pay attention to the beauty around you by opening yourself up to love and discover that the source of love comes not only from our experience of loving another person, friends, pets, God, and the earth. Love is also found in loving you enough to feel filled with the *divine light*. Healing the heart teaches you to trust in the giving and receiving.

6. Let go of controlling all aspects of our life and surrender to the divine universe. Discover that love has no price tag or strings attached. It is simply available everywhere.

CHAPTER III

Finding Beauty in Feelings

"What would it be like if you lived each day,
each breath,
as a work of art in progress?
Imagine that you are a masterpiece unfolding,
every second of every day,
now and now and now and now.
A work of art taking form with each breath.
What would it be like if you lived this way?"

Thomas Crum[13]

1. Feelings and Self-Awareness

The whole process of creating ourselves as prayers to the Divine requires a great deal of self-awareness. Becoming consciously aware of what words we speak, actions we initiate, and thoughts and feelings we have, is a process of self-discovery, which involves paying attention to our feelings.

To build self-awareness requires that we learn to experience ourselves closely without criticism. If in our self-observation, we are highly critical and judgmental, then we are simply recreating the old patterns of self-deprecation and worthlessness. Remembering that we are all students attending Earth School helps us to recognize that we are not perfect and still need lessons about how to develop as a soul. We are really learning that we are not separate and alone but are continuously one with *all there is*. Becoming aware of ourselves, learning to trust ourselves, walking our talk, and loving ourselves just the way we are, are ways to begin to offer ourselves as prayers for the highest good for ourselves, for all concerned, and for all of life everywhere.

To become more aware of ourselves is to open inner eyes to our direct experience of what is unfolding without judgement. "Well, I just saw myself

---

[13]   Thomas F. Crum, *The Magic of Conflict: Turning a Life of Work into a Work of Art* (New York: Simon and Schuster, 1987).

volunteer to teach another class. I am already doing too much. Do I really want to do it? Maybe no one will sign up for the course. Rather than leaving it up to fate, maybe I can find someone else to teach the class." By being aware of our own behavior, we can make conscious choices and take responsibility for our actions.

Do our words and actions match, and therefore, are we trustworthy? "All right, I said I would do it, so I need to honor my commitment. Next time, I will stop and think before I speak. It would probably be a good idea for me to learn to say, 'Thank you very much for asking. I need to take a day to think it over and be sure I can give the class the time it deserves.' That way, I can look at the bigger picture and examine how I am choosing to use my time. Does it match up with my priorities right now?" When we pay attention, we can begin to create new and improved responses.

"Since I have committed myself for now, how can I translate this situation into something that I can get excited about. If I feel better about taking the time to do it, I will probably do a much better job."

How we talk to ourselves is also of utmost importance. I could have said, "You stupid—. There you go again giving away your time. You'll never learn. You are a hopeless idiot." Or, "Let's see how I can weasel out of this one. I'm sure I can find a way to do the class and turn all of the responsibility over to the students. That way, I won't have to do any work. I'll have the best of both worlds, get paid, and be able to do my own work during class." Or, "Now you've done it! How can you possibly be good enough to teach that class? You don't know the material. Everyone will see right through you and know that you are worthless."

Are we constantly putting ourselves down? Are we our own worst enemy? Are we harshly judgmental and critical about ourselves as well as others?

When we are aware of ourselves and catch negativity, we need to learn to stop. Immersing ourselves in negative energy only serves to draw more negative energy to us. We all know people who are constantly complaining about all of the bad things that happen to them. The black cloud seems to follow them wherever they go. It is almost as if these people need bad things in their lives in order to give meaning to their existence.

Sarah used to talk as if she had the worst life on the planet. No one had it quite as hard as she did. Every day, there was a new trauma. Her children were in trouble in school. Her marriage was rocky. Her car was always breaking down. And everyone always heard every last gory detail. She was unable to accept a compliment or a simple gift. For each of these, there was some excuse for why there just happened to be one small exception in her life of trial and tribulation. Sarah did not feel as if she deserved anything except perhaps admiration for living such a difficult life.

Valerie used to worry about everything. She would spend hours thinking through every last detail to be sure she was doing "it" right, whatever "it" happened to be that day. She worried about her health, her children, her job, her marriage, her trips to the grocery store, and her holiday preparations. Would they be good enough? What bad could possibly happen to block her success? She focused on all the bad that could happen in order to prepare herself for the worst. This way, she would never be disappointed.

George, a man in his early thirties, was always concerned with his physical appearance. How could he make himself look perfect? He spent a lot of time working out at the gym, taking supplements, and dreaming of the right implant operation that would make him look just right. He also spent a lot of time fantasizing about sex and finding partners to reassure him that he was still desirable. A lot of time, money, and energy went into convincing him that he was acceptable.

Jeff was always sure that he was going to be fired. As a senior member in his company, he would get very angry about the way he was treated. People, like his boss and younger members of the staff, were not paying him the correct amount of respect. Was there something that they could see about him that he did not know himself? It was very difficult for him to hear anything of value that they did say to him because he had already fixed the dialogue in his mind. Fear ruled him.

Each of these people had no confidence. They didn't trust themselves to make good decisions and their words and actions didn't match. By not loving themselves enough, they were out of balance internally and externally.

As each learned to become aware of his/her own behavior, words and feelings, each was surprised by how out of alignment he/she was with the way he/she really wanted to be. Each set an intention for healing the imbalances and for moving into a more deeply fulfilling life. Sarah, Valerie, and Jeff noticed how much energy they had tied up in creating negative scenario after negative scenario. George and Jeff began to see how much attention they had given to what other people were thinking about them. No wonder they all felt so drained at the end of the day. At times, each had felt that perhaps life wasn't really worth it.

First, each needed to acknowledge his/her feelings. Sarah initially had received a lot of attention for all of her hardships, and she found that she felt compelled to keep creating more. Underneath, she discovered that she was terribly afraid that no one liked her just the way she was. If there were no chaos in her life, would anyone really take the time to notice her? She might disappear or dissolve. That was a very frightening thought.

When Valerie and Jeff paid attention to their worries and worst fears, they began to understand that they had been trained by their parents to always pay attention to the consequences of any behavior. This parental strategy, probably well intentioned, had resulted in paralyzing them. They were too afraid to take risks, too afraid to explore joy and make deep commitments. Life was something to be thoroughly analyzed and planned. There were to be no surprises.

George saw how his drive for the perfect body ended in a complete setup for failure. It was an impossible task that kept him continuously depressed and anxious. He dreamed of a faithful marriage, children, happiness, and contentment. The more he became aware of his feelings, the more he discovered subtle nuances of hurt, anger, and rejection. The more he acknowledged these feelings, the more real he felt. The mask of perfectionism cracked and fell away.

By shifting their focus to the positive, they each learned how to reshape their sentences. They could reward themselves with kind words, spoken out of the true knowledge of what it had taken to get to that point. Often, recognizing and speaking an internal "Good job!" or "You look nice today!" or "I really liked the part where I could feel my heart open and be very loving. Next time, I would like to be more vocal about expressing what I am feeling." Rather than beating themselves up for making mistakes, they could take the time to learn from them and experiment with new internal dialogues that were supportive and self-affirming. Change actually began to happen more and more easily.

They learned to think of themselves like mothers and fathers who honored and respected their children and who wanted to see them to be the best they could be. By speaking with care, respect, and understanding, they brought more balance and harmony into their lives.

When you were a child, the building of your self-esteem was in the hands of the adults in your world. When they praised you, you knew you had done well and had value. It felt good to be acknowledged for your accomplishments. If only negative comments were given, you knew you weren't good enough, and you were left in a quandary because you had no idea what was expected of you. As an adult, it is your job to create your own self-esteem. If you are lucky, you may have a good work situation, where your contributions are acknowledged and valued. In most work situations, little feedback of any value is given and you are left on your own. As an adult, different from when you were a child, you have more cognitive abilities, more control over your life and choices. Speaking kindly to yourself, acknowledging your accomplishments, and recognizing your behavior as having value are ways to enhance your self-esteem.

When you do something, do you take responsibility with the words that you speak? Do your words and actions have integrity? If your words and actions match over time, then you are a trustworthy person. You need to be able to trust yourself as well as others. I had a client, who was starting his own business. He told me that he had gotten very angry with a supplier who had repeatedly sent the wrong expensive item. My client was beside himself because some "idiot," who was incapable of listening, was holding up his own work. He finally ended up talking with the supplier and getting it straightened out, but he confessed that he told a little white lie. He told the boss that a smaller item had been shipped and that he would accept it only if he would give him some of his money back. In my client's mind, he deserved this money because of the delay in his valuable time, not to mention all of the aggravation he had had to suffer.

I suggested to him that he needed to be careful, since his intention was to serve the higher good through his business. If he stopped and thought about it from an energy viewpoint, he might see that he had set up his business with a clear intention. The clarity of his intention generated an energy or aura of honesty and integrity around his business that was helping to build his good reputation in the community so that people trusted him. "A little white lie" brought in a very different kind of energy; one that would begin to act corrosively. He might find it easy to justify the next little lie, and then the next, until where would his personal integrity be? He needed to make a conscious choice about which reality he wanted to create.

2. Using a Journal

Very often, writing in a journal helps to heighten the awareness of your own process. Writing down thoughts and feelings gets them outside of you. If you are confused, writing out of your confusion can give you a different perspective. You have emptied your mind and put the words on a piece of paper. This process gives you the opportunity to see your thoughts more clearly. It may help you to sort them through with a sense of greater objectivity.

When I was thirty, I began a master's program in dance/movement therapy. This was my first introduction into the field of psychology. I'll never forget the day a woman in the class leaned over to me and said, "You know, the body has feelings."

Amazed at such a concept, I responded, "You have to be kidding me." Well, I had a lot to learn. As a dancer, I knew the physical body intimately, but I did not have a clue about my emotions. I was so out of touch with my feelings that I did not even have a vocabulary to describe my experience. I began by drawing, giving each of the colors or shapes a voice. Then I would use words to describe the colors, shapes, or images. As I wrote out the words, the feelings emerged, and I began to connect with them.

I also turned to my body a lot. Maybe I was feeling stiff somewhere or had pain. Again, I would begin by giving that part of my body a voice. By describing in my journal what I was physically feeling, I began to discover what I was feeling emotionally.

Here is an example of how a dialogue might be written out. This occurred as I was writing this section. The journal continues to be a useful tool! I first begin describing what I am aware of. "My left shoulder is killing me. It feels as if there is a burning sensation emanating from under my collarbone outward towards my shoulder joint. It makes my whole left arm feel limp, powerless. For several days, I have tried to loosen it with exercise and warm it with a hot shower. Nothing has changed. The pain actually began several weeks ago when I was sick. The rest of me is feeling much better, but not my shoulder. What is going on?"

Then the dialogue begins with my shoulder, "I am reminding you to keep limp and loose. You constantly want to take on too much. You need to slow down and focus your attention on that which is most important to you."

I reply, "Yes, I agree with you. I need to keep loose. And since I have returned from vacation, haven't I been doing just that? My schedule is simpler. I am eating and exercising in a healthy way. I am back to doing my meditations and prayers in the morning. And I am having a very good time doing the writing I need to do. What do you mean by keeping limp? Limp feels powerless. I don't like that."

"Limp means your left side is still out of balance. Please pay attention to the ways you can nurture yourself better. Pay attention to receiving from others and the universe what you need. You are not here to do it all by yourself! It would also be helpful to get back into some other creative activity as well as the writing." (Just as I am typing this part about the creative activity, the pain in my shoulder begins to diminish. That is a very good clue that getting involved in a creative activity is an important part of the solution.)

"I am very willing to do something fun and creative. Watercolors come to mind, or making a leather pouch for my friend. I am also aware that there are a lot of demands on my time and that I need to be much more careful with my choices. A lot of new clients have called in the last several days. I need to set limits. Balancing work, play, creativity, writing, and my own personal spiritual work is very important and challenging." The left side is associated with the feminine, and that also means taking the time to do nothing but simply be present to the moment in deep silence. When life gets busy, that is the part that seems to go first. When I was sick, I was forced to do nothing. Now that my energy is back, it is harder to choose to do nothing. "Shoulder, I thank you for this reminder. I request that you release your grip on me, and let me bring my life back into balance in peace and beauty."

This written dialogue, inspired by the pain in my shoulder, helped me come to a greater understanding of what was going on inside. I had no idea at the beginning of the writing what words would come out. If the pain in my shoulder persisted, I would have needed to go back to the drawing board and pick up the dialogue where I had left off, because my shoulder had more to teach me.

Sometimes people get very confused with their feelings. Or put a high value on some feelings and devalue others. It is right to be loving, and wrong to be angry. It is imperative to remember that there are no rights or wrongs or good or bad feelings. They are what they are, plain and simple. You may not like what you are feeling. What is most important is that you acknowledge your feelings, feel them, name them, own them, and take responsibility for them. Only then do they begin to shift and change to something more comfortable.

Sometimes, I really enjoy writing poetry as a way of expressing deep feelings. This poem was written at the painful end of a relationship. It felt deeply satisfying and freeing to write the following words:

My body is dulled by a lover gone bad.
Fingers run across silken skin
feeling softness there.
There is no thrill,
no echo reaching down into my depths,
awakening the slumbering serpent.
My dark moist cave lies barren
emitting only sighs of cold air.
Gone is the heat of passion.
Gone is the dance of eternal rhythms.
Gone is the sweet surrender
of a heart wide open.
My body is dulled by a lover gone bad.

You may be furious with someone. Feel the feeling, acknowledge it, and maybe even briefly entertain a fantasy about what you want to do to that person. This does not mean that you have to act out on what you are feeling. Allow the anger to resonate through your body. Feel the color, texture, and energy of it. Then allow that energy to move out of your body, letting it dissipate and disappear, so that you are no longer holding the fantasy or the feeling. Sometimes it is helpful to write a letter to the person with whom you are very angry as a means of releasing the energy. You can choose to send it or not. The writing is primarily for you to work through your feelings and release them. Hanging on to this negative energy in your body can lead to extra stress and eventually disease. When the relationship that I mentioned was ending, I wrote a lot in my journal. Some entries were poems, and some were paragraphs. I also wrote a number of letters to the man I had been involved with. Some I read to him in person, some I sent, and some I did not. It was a very helpful way for me to sort through the many different feelings I was having at the time. And it was a very helpful way to learn what I needed to learn, to express what I was feeling, and to let go of the relationship.

3. Communicating Feelings

A primary gift that comes from being a human is that our experiences are enriched through feelings of all sorts. Life becomes rich brocade instead of plain muslin. You get to choose. If we dampen feelings at one end of the spectrum, all feelings are diminished. We cannot expect to go through life only feeling happy. That happiness will become hollow and meaningless without access to the full range of feelings being expressed.

If you deny your feelings, they usually come sneaking back in a lot less controlled manner. When an anorexic client of mine was mad at her mother or me, she starved herself. When couples build resentments over the little stuff, like whose turn it is to clean the bathroom or pick up the dirty underwear on the bedroom floor or being late and do not communicate with each other, a crack begins to develop between them. Some explode when the sack on the camel's back is stuffed so full it can't hold another straw. Names get shouted and irretrievable statements are made that result in less and less caring and intimacy. "You lazy so and so, you never help around the house!" It might have been simpler and less damaging to say, "Would you please do the dishes tonight." But if this is at the long end of a series of unexpressed annoyances, the tirade begins, feelings get hurt, and nothing gets resolved.

I saw a woman who was experiencing considerable distress because she felt ignored and dismissed by her husband. Allegedly, she was upset because he had refused to call his brother-in-law (her brother) back to tell him that he would not be coming to his bachelor's party. For some reason, he didn't feel it was necessary. She was trying desperately to keep the already strained family relationships peaceful, and he hadn't taken the time to listen to her feelings about the family situation. In her effort to get him to understand her position, she explained more and more. In his effort to get her to stop from "going on and on," he stated his position more and more loudly. Before either of them knew what was happening, he was yelling and she was crying because she felt as if her feelings didn't count. They were both threatening to end the marriage; all over whether or not he should call his brother-in-law back.

It was really very simple. She wanted her feelings acknowledged. She knew he had a right to his own opinion, and so did she. "Please listen to what I am feeling." Expressing feelings and having those feelings received and acknowledged is very important. When you respond by saying in your own words, "This is what I am hearing you say . . . ," it does not mean that you necessarily agree. It only means that you are hearing what is being expressed. You are acknowledging the feelings of another. After putting what the other has said in his own words, "I am hearing that you are feeling upset because I don't want to call your brother back," his wife might tell him that that is part of it and explain a little more. Her husband would continue, "Okay, you are also afraid that he will be angry with us and you don't want any more fights between us and your family." After this process of clarification, when he has understood her feelings, only then is it his turn to reply. And the procedure of listening, acknowledging, clarifying, and responding now goes to the other person. So many couples get into big trouble by not taking the time to listen and acknowledge each other's feelings. Often there is the misconception, "We've been together for four years . . . if he loved me, he should know what I am feeling." The number of years two people have spent together does not help either of them develop mind-reading skills.

Sometimes you may find yourself so angry or upset about something that you need time to regain control and clarity before you respond. You do not have to immediately tell the other what you are feeling. It may be necessary to take a few minutes, or an hour, before you say anything in order to stop and think things through before speaking or acting. This is not always easy. Taking three deep breathes, or counting to ten are good techniques for slowing yourself down in order to think before you respond. Some people use visualizing a stop sign or red light to stop them from jumping headlong into something that they will regret later. Another possibility is to establish ahead of time that the "time out" hand signal means "I need a break." Using a creative way to pause gives you a chance to step back, get a helpful perspective, and to be sure that what you are about to say is what you really want to say. Don't just walk away. Be respectful and inform your partner that you will be back to continue the conversation so he or she is not feeling abandoned or dismissed. You also need to be willing to relinquish the pleasure you find in fighting, being right, or whatever else keeps you engaged.

Being honest about what you are feeling is crucial. It does not help to lie to yourself or another person. If you are very angry with your wife and want to get a divorce, be straight. In ending my first marriage, I still cared for my husband and didn't want to hurt his feelings, but I wanted out of the marriage for a number of reasons. I tried to do it softly and gently. As I look back, it must have felt like Chinese water torture to him. Little by little, I was letting him go. It would have been so much simpler if I had been honest. The bottom line was I wanted out and he did not. Yes, it was very hurtful. There was no way around it. The clarity of being honest would have been very helpful and perhaps less hurtful in the long run.

Feelings are an aspect of your reality. They are an expression of you and are both beautiful and scary. They are where your passion, power, and humanness lie. They are where you touch God. It is very powerful to be in touch with your feelings and to connect with another by being honest about your feelings. It is very powerful to feel another's feelings, but always know that they come through the filter of your own life experience. It is important to check it out with the other person by asking, "Is this what you are experiencing?" I remember a time when I was dating a man who was reading a book about women. He thought he was being very insightful when he told me he knew exactly what I was feeling as a result of this book. His comment made me furious because he had failed to ask me and had gone to a secondary source. I felt invisible.

Make an assessment about the safety of expressing what it is that you are feeling. Most people probably err on the side of not speaking up enough and prefer to hide their thoughts. This goes back to trust. Do you trust the other person enough to honor your feelings? Do you trust yourself enough to be honest? If there is a history of violent behavior, it might be safer to write a letter and then decide whether to send it or not.

When we make a commitment to do something or set an intention, our actions need to follow suit, not just once or twice, but over time. We need to take full responsibility for the actions we make and the words we speak. If I am writing a book about living life as a prayer, I need to be living my life in a prayerful way. "Do as I say and not as I do" results in no integrity and no respect. The most powerful teachers are those who embody what they are teaching. The more you stop and pay attention to your own feelings, actions, and words, the more your awareness will become heightened. Paying attention to your actions, words and body makes it easier to know yourself and to express your feelings with confidence.

Here are words from the Council of ADRON that came in a reading with Starfeather for Sue, whom we met when she was setting her intention to come into wholeness and well-being. She was asking the council how she could find balance and harmony within herself, how she could open her heart to God's love, and how she could discover her purpose. The response went something like this.

"First comes trust. Trust in yourself and the journey you are embarking on. God is already in you and around you and cannot be found out there somewhere. God can be found in your own self, in your **feeling** self.

"First connect fully with yourself. The time has come to face the shadows, for they are the teachers and healers. Find a safe way to look at it all and to grieve the losses as well as remember the joys. It is all part of your story. Speak from your heart. Connecting with your deep self will enable you to see the world and your family through different eyes.

"We would suggest that you create a ceremony for yourself, not a birthday party per se but a celebration on becoming a *wise woman,* an *elder.* Your experiences have great value. Begin to share your emotional self with others. Create a special place in your home that is your 'church.' Create an altar to God by bringing a candle, a crystal, a photo, and/or a flower to this place. Select things that you consider sacred. Find writings of truth, such as 'God is Love,' 'Peace is within me.' We suggest that you search for these sayings outside of the Bible. Spend time at this altar. Say hello every morning and begin your day simply by being thankful. As you leave your 'church,' carry the energy of it into your day. Begin to see the earth as a living being full of love and as a presence of God.

"You may want to *ask* for teachers to come to you who can help you. Group prayer is always of value. Once you feel connected and in love again with your *sacred self,* you can begin the true work of an elder, which is to give back to the earth and all her people for the greater good.

"Your work is good. **Expand your feeling of it.** Every time you hear a baby or touch a child (the woman for whom the reading is being done is a medical assistant in an OB-GYN practice), know that you are an expression of God's love for that one, as that one is for you. As you go deep within, discover your *beauty* and let it *shine* out for all to see. Ignite the fire of passion for life within your own self. Love. Sing. Dance. And remember *you are a goddess.*"

These beautiful words remind us that our feelings are the key to embracing the divine. For a long while now, I have gone out in the morning to the pray-place, a special spot in the woods near my house. I have set up a medicine wheel and cloth flags that mark the four directions, each of which carry special teachings. Here I sit for a long while taking in the beauty that is all around me. As I begin to say or sing, drum or dance prayers of gratitude that come as expressions of feelings from my heart, the more I feel filled with the grace of God. The more love I feel, the more joy I feel. It is very helpful for me to come here first thing in the morning, to take the time to notice the beauty, to feel my feelings and to express them.

4. Moving through Fear into Grace

Do not fear what you
do not understand,
instead seek to learn.
Do not be one who turns
Away from awareness in fear,
for there is much
being held in the balance.

Mentor
Meredith Young[14]

I was in the surgeon's office waiting to hear the results of a pathology report. I had discovered that—like so many others on the planet at this time—something on my body wasn't quite right. A month ago, I had thought that a bump on my skin had been a chigger bite. This was not so unusual. I live in the woods and sit outside at my pray-place every morning. This had been a particularly virulent chigger summer. But this little red bump did not itch. It also brought back memories of my mother right before her death. She was dying of throat cancer, which had spread throughout her body and began manifesting itself all over her chest in large red bumps. My bump was not nearly so big, but it had that same look.

The initial appointment was with a skin specialist, who couldn't see me for another two months. I felt an inner urgency that made me call a surgeon. He removed it quickly without any apparent alarm, so I was not really worried. I was just glad to have this extra piece off of my body.

The surgeon was away on vacation, so his assistant gave me the results of the routine pathology report and informed me that it was a melanoma and not the primary site. I was very surprised. I knew that didn't sound good. Not being a cancer expert, I asked as many questions as I could think of at the moment. She looked my whole body over carefully for indications of other lesions and found

14   Meredith Young, *Agartha: The Essential Guide to Personal Transformation in the New Era* (Ballantine Books, 1989).

none. The advice was to see an eye specialist and to have a colonoscopy done, because those tissues were possibilities for primary sites. The extracted tissue had been sent on to another lab for a second opinion.

I am a very healthy person. I am a dancer/choreographer who has done yoga for years. I had been vegetarian for a very long time. I garden organically and co-creatively, raising high-quality food. I do massage, acupuncture, and other energy work on a regular basis, maintaining a good wellness program. I see myself as a whole person and have worked to connect my body, mind, and spirit in the present moment. I have paid a lot of attention to keep myself healthy. This was a little more excitement than I had bargained for, so I was upset. Cancer did not fit in this lifestyle, or so I thought.

I decided to get as much information as I could. There are lots of ways to gather information; mine is mostly to consult with people that I respect and to check into my own feelings and inner knowing. I needed to feel in control of the process and, at the same time, give full consideration to new information. I went home and telephoned a good friend who was a nurse-practitioner. She explained a little more to me. I called my sister, Starfeather, to ask for a reading on my body with the Council of ADRON. She is guided to draw people as light and energy and could receive information from this group intelligence about the state of my health. I was curious about what they would have to say.

I went for a long walk in the woods in between clients and prayed out loud to whoever was listening. I felt wonderful, full of the love of the Creator, full of grace. My body felt strong and clear and healthy. The trees reached out their green-cloaked beauty. The earth held me gently to her body. The birds sang sweetly, and the soft breeze brought moist, earthy smells. My being was radiant. I knew that there was no more cancer in my body.

That night, when my sister connected with me, I felt a cloud of pink energy hover over me. I was filled with love and felt intensely beautiful. This energy moved through me, thoroughly scanning my body. My sister, who was on the opposite side of the continent, reported later that she had prayed hard to remove her ego, her attachment and love for me, so that this group could do its work unhindered and the reading would not be her wishful thinking. This was not an easy task because we are very close. This was what they wrote.

"This is ADRON. We come in service to this *beloved one*. Yes, this is ADRON. We have just been with Claybasket (my Native American spirit name), yes. We find *no* evidence of any *imbalance*. There is no primary source of which you call cancer. This body is clear, we repeat, clear. We repeat, clear.

"STAND STRONG in your belief, it is the basis of your reality, and it can shift by outside influences. All sights are clear.

"Your soul's purpose does not change according to the winds or the news in today's paper. Your soul's purpose is a constant. Your awareness of the full picture is the only thing that changes. Your emotional body is the only aspect of your whole self that needs attunement at this time and understandably so. You have experienced a shock to your system. This experience may help you to remember never to forget even for *one moment WHO YOU ARE*. We are not here to play a game with you or to cast you into hell and leave you there. You have died and been REBORN. Perhaps what the test saw was a residue of this. You are so loved, dear one, so *cherished*. This experience can only deepen your COMPASSION and your *trust* in your knowing. Do not put all of your skills aside for one lab test. Yes, you may want new glasses, contact lenses. Find a conscious eye healer/worker. Do not be afraid. Cradle that little one and love her. She is *not* your mother.

"WRITE NOW."

ADRON

I felt very affirmed and supported. I sang and danced many prayers of gratitude. Once again, I felt filled with the love of the Creator and slept well that night.

The next day, I had an appointment with the eye doctor. After careful examination, he reported no evidence of abnormality. After consulting with him, I decided not to go with contacts. That day, I also had my seventh Rolfing appointment. A series of ten completes the whole treatment. She mentioned that because the bump had come after we had begun our work, there was a possibility that it was old stuff being released by the body, which was not an uncommon occurrence. I knew that this was usually the case with old unresolved emotional issues. Often those emotions held deep within cellular memory are released during deep tissue work. Maybe it manifested physically. This was interesting as a possible explanation, particularly because the red bump had been so clearly associated with my mother.

I waited a long time for the second pathology report. It hadn't come before a joyous week at the beach with a house full of friends. I carried on as usual. My friend Phebe and I spent time each day studying Machaelle Small Wright's new book on co-creative science. That week, I had an especially wonderful time getting up at 4:30 every morning, going down to the beach while it was still dark to sit and pray. The star system Orion was lying on her side. Pleiades danced high overhead as Sirius, a radiant blue, slipped over the horizon. The last quarter moon cupped the early-morning sky. And then very slowly, imperceptibly at first, the first blush of light would appear as if by some great mysterious magic. Gradually, as the light grew, low-lying clouds would become laced with brilliant pinks and gold, which shifted slowly to grays and whites. In a moment of utmost drama, the rim of red liquid light would surface on the horizon, gradually elongating a path of shimmering yellows, pinks, and reds on the gray green water. The ocean, whose waves had been chanting a song that was the same and always different, turned to robin's egg, blue with sparkles riding out with each wave. What a glory to behold the rising of the sun!

The beach and friends had been incredibly relaxing, but the world spun at a fast pace when I returned. After a week, I remembered to call for another appointment. This report was even worse than the first: metastatic adnocarcenoma. The surgeon was very serious and was not the least bit interested in my assessment. There were lethal tumors somewhere in my body that would need to come out. No, he had never heard of any cases where they found nothing. I realized later that he would be most familiar with the existence of things he had to cut out. He told me that there needed to be a whole series of tests run to find them and tried to set up an appointment for me with the oncologist in his practice. I took this name from his secretary but told her I would make the appointment myself. I wanted to consult with my friend and make my own decision about whom I would see.

Another shock to my emotional body! I cried. I sang. I prayed and talked aloud to whomever else was listening and myself. While this was difficult, it still did not resonate or feel accurate. Maybe there had been a mix-up in the lab, and those tissues were not mine. The two reports seemed so different. Surprisingly, I felt no fear. I was still confident that I was clear, even though I had wobbled a little after experiencing the intensity of the surgeon. I called my friend for more information and advice on a good oncologist. She steered me to someone, who set up an appointment for the following day. I went on to a full day of clients.

At the end of the day, I talked with my sister for support and called in the medical assistance team that works with me. This is a co-creative process that has been devised by Machaelle Small Wright[15] and nature to help with personal health issues. (See the chapter on creating your own personal MAP team for more information.) I have been working this way for a number of years, with many surprising successes. Last year, when I was going through a particularly difficult time emotionally, they would help me sleep at night and help keep me as balanced as possible so that I could work through the issues I needed to and learn the lessons that were the gift of that time. There have been other times when I have felt on the edge of the flu and, with their help, felt completely recovered the next morning, while others around me were debilitated for a week or more. At this point, I wanted them to scan my body and give me a second opinion. Again, the verdict was that I was clear.

I also decided to call a friend who is a Reiki master. Would she please just triple check? We met at the pray-place several days later and reviewed the situation. She found the body clear and the mind in conflict. We talked about my practice as a psychologist. Was I bringing my full truth to my clients, discussing with them new ways of healing, of praying, of finding the balance within their body, mind,

---

[15] Machaelle Small Wright, *MAP: The Co-creative White Brotherhood Medical Assistance Program* (Virginia: Perelandra, Ltd., 1995).

and spirit much the way I am talking about things in this book. I have been encouraged to do healing work as a shamanic healer. This is definitely outside of the purview of my license as a psychologist. Yes, I have been much more open with my ideas in treatment, but no, I had not done journey work for clients. These were certainly issues I needed to think more about.

The next day, I began to write in my journal about this experience at the suggestion of my friend Suzy. I realized that I had been very annoyed at the interference this whole event was causing in my life. I had so much on my plate. This was like a thorn I wanted to pull out of my side and throw away. I knew I was clear and healthy, why did I have to keep bothering with more. Apparently, the universe had something else in mind. This experience was certainly very present, very front and center in my life. I had better turn around and embrace it. Writing about my experience would help me sort through the issues and feelings.

What were the lessons here? Well, I was writing a book on healing the heart in order to live life as a prayer. Even though there was no resonance of fear for me, I could see how easy it would be to forget what I knew and give myself over to the "higher authority," the well-meaning doctors. It would be easy for me to take the "C" word as a sentence of death. That is what we have been taught. It would be easy to get caught up in all of the fears associated with this disease.

Instead, my experience was one of feeling filled with the love of the Great Mystery, of God, of grace. I felt full of health, vitality, and radiance. Maybe this was part of the truth I was being asked to embrace. The writing helped me clarify these thoughts.

The next day, I had my last Rolfing appointment with Debra. It was a celebration of three or four months worth of good work, which had resulted in some postural shifts, as well as a clarity and freedom of movement that I had never experienced before. I truly felt as if I were opening up to new aspects of myself with an expanded connection to creation.

From there, I went to my first appointment with the oncologist. I instantly felt good about him and his assistant. He examined closely both lab reports, took a health history, asked a number of pertinent questions, and listened carefully to my answers. He also examined me. He was respectful, both in giving me his opinion and listening to my assessment. I told him that having grown up in an alcoholic household, I was well aware of the dance between denial and this inner knowing. There seemed to me to be a fine line between not wanting to know if cancer was there by putting it out of conscious awareness and knowing from the core of my being that I was a radiantly healthy human being. I wanted to be responsible and work with him.

We talked over options. He was aware of the fact that I had no insurance, and I could hear him taking that into consideration. There were a number of tests that could be used, some very expensive and some not so expensive. He wanted to begin by sending the tissue to another lab, one that he had confidence would run all of the necessary tests. Apparently, they had not examined all of the possibilities, and I found out that it was "not so easy to properly diagnose" tissue. We agreed to begin there and take one step at a time. He said that there was no doubt that the tissue that was removed had malignant cells in it and that there were clear margins of two centimeters surrounding it. Apparently, the surgeon had not suspected cancer by the way in which the incision was made. At the very end, he told me that he did not think that we would find any more evidence of cancer.

While discussing my evolving situation with my Crones group (a group of seven women who meet monthly to share support, love, and healing with each other), I realized I was receiving another lesson. I understood what it felt like to truly KNOW something. The best way I could describe my experience was as if I were a crystal bell that was being sounded, the tone was resonating through my being with an astounding clarity and beauty.

This level of knowing had come to me hard won. Just a year and a half ago, I found out that the man I had been living with for six and a half years had been involved with another woman for three of those years. It had begun for him three weeks after he had made a public commitment to me at his own instigation in front of our friends at the closing ceremony of the Good Medicine Society's spring gathering. The long and the short of it was that I had had a number of intuitive hits during the course of those three years, had often confronted him directly, and had put aside my intuition to believe his lies. Evidently, I hadn't been ready to face my fears, or even, perhaps, myself.

All along, my intuition had been jiggling like the doll in the pocket of Vassalisa. This is a wonderful Russian folktale retold by Clarissa Pinkola Estés. Briefly, on her deathbed, Vassalisa's mother presents her with a doll to carry always in her pocket. She is to call on this doll whenever she is in difficulty, since her mother will no longer be around to guide her. Time passes and her father remarries a woman who, at first, appears to love Vassalisa dearly. Gradually, she works it around to where the child, always caring and wishing to please, is doing most of the work for the mother and her two natural daughters. Eventually, they come to hate the young girl, who is nice to them no matter how badly they treat her. They send her off to the home of the Baba Yaga, the most powerful of witches, to bring back fire to light the hearth, which they have secretly extinguished. Of course, they think they have sent her off to her death.

When the frightened Vassalisa finds herself alone in the forest, lost in the middle of the night, she begins to entertain the idea that these women have not had her best interest at heart. When she comes to a fork in the road, she asks out loud, "Which way am I suppose to turn?" The long-forgotten doll in her pocket jiggles the answer that leads her down the path of growth and knowledge to Baba Yaga's doorstep. Here she is tested over and over, and with the assistance of the doll in her pocket, she overcomes the odds and is rewarded by the gift of fire, or conscious awareness. Upon returning home, she takes charge of her life, always guided by the inner knowing of her powerful intuition.

The lesson offered to me was much the same. I had given too much and been satisfied with too little. I had settled for a certain kind of comfort, devoid of passion. Over and over again, I had ignored the doll in the pocket, or let my partner convince me that I was asking for too much. This was the hard way I learned that my intuition was a very valuable source of knowledge.

When the third pathology report came back, it was a completely different kind of cancer: primary cutaneous lymphoma. According to my nurse-practitioner friend, if you have to have cancer, this is the kind to have because the cure rate is very high. While this was affirming, I wondered if we were simply taking the best pick of the three different diagnoses. Apparently, the third lab was the definitive one in the country, with experts in each kind of cancer. It still amazes me that there can be such big mistakes made in such a grave situation.

Right after receiving the third report, I went to visit my father. As usual, I went outside for my morning meditation, prayer, and to greet the sun with song. This time, I was on Cape Cod Bay. The morning was bright, and the tidal waters were pulled way out, revealing drifts of sand on which a myriad of seagoing birds had landed. It occurred to me that I wanted to do the same as I had been recommending to my clients. Why not take the Rolfer, the acupuncturist, and the Reiki master with me to see the oncologist. I wanted him to hear from the other practitioners who have been working with me. Each of them had experienced my body from a different perspective. I felt that he might have more information from which to make a decision if he talked with the team of people who were working with me.

On the morning before the oncology appointment, I saw Tess, the acupuncturist. She was going to check my lymph system and see if there were any imbalances. This would be another important piece of information, since apparently, the type of cancer I had had involved the lymph system. As we always did, we began the session with a prayer, and I called in the medical assistance team to help guide the treatment and augment the healing work. She says that sometimes she can feel their presence and feels moved to do some points that she would not ordinarily do. This morning, she strengthened the thymus and spleen. After she finished the two points on the wrists, I felt as if I had two globes of light surrounding each one, like two magnificent bracelets. The pulses were strong and healthy. She had checked her notes and remarked on the husband/wife imbalance that had been present when the first bump had surfaced. I was reminded how out of sorts I had felt at the time, as if my whole electrical system was being realigned.

I had scheduled some craniosacral-energy work[16] as well. Again the MAP team was invited in and prayers were spoken. The cranial-sacral pulses were

---

[16]   Craniosacral-energy work focuses on the release of negative energy in the craniosacral system, which includes all of the soft tissue in the body.

strong and vibrant, but there was an excess of energy on the right shoulder and upper rib cage, right where the surgery had been done. Images of my arm being pulled out of the socket, as if I was being swung by the arm, came to me. Julie drained the energy, as I toned into that space[17]. It felt as if she were reconstructing me. Cords of light were helping to reconnect my arm to my body. An old injury to the muscle running from the spine under the scapula was sensitized and then released. My shoulder felt brand new.

Now, I was on to the oncologist. Before introducing the acupuncturist, the Rolfer and the Reiki master, I made my intention clear to the oncologist. I wanted us to operate as a healing team, bringing together vital information from a variety of perspectives. This would help us all to be on the same page, so to speak, and would offer me the opportunity to make the best judgment on which of the next steps would I want to take.

He was gracious and listened as each one explained her orientation to the body and to my treatment. He discussed several different tests that he would recommend and the information that each would provide. I told him that I would give his recommendation serious consideration. I discussed the options with my treatment team and decided that I had enough information and would not proceed further. I let him know of my decision in a letter.

I had not really discussed my situation with anyone in my family with the exception of my sister because, at first, the diagnosis had not been clear. I didn't want to get people unnecessarily upset. I did rely on close friends for support because it was important to talk about it. I didn't want to create a lot of negative energy of worry around me. Now, I was ready to talk with them. My oldest son, Yosha, was particularly upset because he was worried and feared that I was not getting the information that I needed in a timely manner. He did speak with the oncologist. That helped somewhat.

Needless to say, this was continuing to be a powerful learning experience. It was essential to face the full range of feelings that I experienced and allow them to resonate fully through my body. Talking to friends, writing, creating a team of healers and doctors to help, taking control of my own treatment, praying and facing the fears—all were important things to do. I believe very strongly in a partnership model. I wanted to share in the decision-making process. I wanted to choose the best doctor and the right treatment for my body, mind, and spirit. I also wanted multiple resources that looked at me from a variety of perspectives, with the hopes that a more complete picture would be discerned.

---

[17]   Toning is done by singing or humming a single note. In this case, the note was hummed while I pictured in my mind's eye the anatomical structure of the part of the body I wanted to send the sound to. This set up an internal vibration that could be felt in that part of the body. It was deeply relaxing.

I did not want to cave in to a place of fear. I certainly needed to acknowledge my fears, and I needed to let them move through me and out, not hanging on. I had to feel my own truth, not through stubbornness or denial or ignorance, but by accessing my own inner knowing. I needed to remain grounded by staying in touch with the earth by walking, gardening, sitting in the woods, and talking with nature. All of this may sound certifiably crazy, but I am convinced that we have a preponderance of resources available to us from both the "real" three-dimensional world and from the spirit world. We are never alone, and we are loved beyond measure. It is up to us to open the doors, acknowledge these resources, and ask them in to accompany us on our life's journey. The more we recognize this abundance, the more full we feel. This is tapping into the natural flow of loving energy.

A little more than a year later, two more bumps were cut from my body. Once again, I felt free and clear, and there was obviously a process going on in my body that needed closer examination. This examination involved not only my body, but also my basic philosophy about life. The kind of cancer that I had is apparently rare; found in only four out of a million people. Moreover, I didn't fit the usual profile. And my body was still generating cancer cells. I reached out for emotional support from family and friends. I made the necessary doctors' appointments and included my extended team. Again, I was in charge of my healing, and I had to go further than I did the year before.

I met with my friend John, who is a doctoral student in pharmacology. He works with cancer patients at the local hospital. He and I went over a chapter that he had found in a textbook that discussed the particular kind of cancer that I had. We reviewed the pathology reports. John found that there were thirteen protocols on this particular kind of cancer being run at NIH (National Institutes of Health). Again, I wanted to have as much knowledge as I could before I saw the oncologist. I knew now that there were a lot of medical resources available.

I decided to consult with a medical intuitive. This person works with a spirit guide who specializes in diseases in the body. My sister was encouraging me to do this because she didn't feel that the Council of ADRON was as well versed in this area. When I talked with a medical intuitive, she suggested that I think of the cancer as originating from an imprint on my DNA and that my DNA was shifting and changing.

When I spoke with the Council of ADRON, they didn't like the use of the word imprint. Using such a powerful word implies a certain permanence and gives this gene on my DNA a feeling of immutability. My impression was that they wanted me to understand that even the coding on the DNA can be changed. After all, the DNA is made up of molecules, which are basically patterns of energy: moveable and transmutable. I was reminded of the ability of matter to change even when we consider it a solid form. The energy in my body that has generated these cancer cells could be transformed.

The intuitive suggested that these forms can shift and change as I raise the vibrational frequency in my body through various forms of vibrational healing, like homeopathy, acupuncture, Reiki, flower essences, or toning. I could use prayer, song, dance, and drumming to embrace these cancer cells and the gene on the strand of DNA. I did not want do battle with it. That would bring a negative energy to it. Loving my body and feeling filled with the grace of the Divine created an incompatibility with the vibrational frequency of the cancer. The cancer, in a certain sense, would have to shift its energy to stay with me, or it would have to leave.

I have been cautioned not to call myself a cancer patient. This, too, lends power to the disease. There is a fine line to be recognized between denial and working with my body to strengthen my immune and lymph systems and to focus attention on creating a loving environment throughout the entirety of my being. I had been told that the healing will come through the use of vibrational medicine and the tracking of the disease through allopathic (Western) medicine. I needed to be in my body with awareness in order to notice the balances and imbalances.

I needed to stay in touch with my emotional reality. I was running the gamut. While I had no intention of dying from this disease, I considered that death was sitting on my left shoulder. If I was to have only a short time left in three-dimensional reality, was there anything I would do differently right now? I searched through the ways I spent my days and felt pretty satisfied. I could always use more time for creative projects, working in the garden, being with friends and family, or simply being with the earth. I needed to seriously consider these changes.

I set the intention to embark on a heart-centered healing journey that would teach me what I needed to know in order to continue my life at my best. I put this in the form of a prayer: "Creator of all things, help me find all of the resources I need in order to co-create a healing journey from the heart that is in alignment with my desire to serve to the best of my ability. I am available. Ho, Mitakque Oyasin." I celebrated the curious twists and turns of life that forge us in the fire of possibilities, creating who we are always becoming.

I also didn't think that I had done anything wrong, that I was a bad person, or that bad things happen to good people. What is, is. I live a very balanced and beautiful life, and I had more cancer cells in my body. I couldn't naively deny that fact. I had set my intention. I proceeded step by step in the present moment, paying a great deal of attention to my feelings, to my body, and the information that I continued to gather. I was grateful for the love and support I received from family and friends.

I decided to take the necessary tests to see if my lymph system was involved. If the lymph system was involved, this would mean a much more serious progression of the disease. Four more months went by when another bump appeared. I now had insurance, so I was free to run the tests. After the CAT scans were read, I was quickly sent to the Washington Hospital Center because apparently one of the lymph glands behind my sternum was swollen. This was not a good sign. This would indicate a more advanced stage of the disease.

I continued my complementary therapies, increasing the numbers of appointments. Again, this information was very unnerving, but when I visualized my lymph system, I saw streams of sparkling white light. I held strong in my belief that the bumps were a residue of past issues currently resolved. I came across a passage in my journal that I had written earlier about the relationship that had ended. It was written prior to any diagnosis of cancer. "And we drifted further apart. I was opening to myself, to my destiny, and to my spirituality. I was dancing my dance with the light and the dark. While I was focused on healing the earth, people, and myself, a cancer began to grow in my bed." That was interesting! The time I was referring to was six years earlier when those cancer cells would have been forming.

At the Washington Hospital Center, I was met by a very nice patient advocate who asked me how I was feeling. She took a brief history and told me about all of the resources they had available. She showed me their library of materials and said, "I want to show you this room. In here, we have wigs for only fifteen dollars, where they normally sell for ninety-five to one hundred." I was stunned. I was not prepared for wigs. It felt very inappropriate and out of context.

By the time I saw the doctor who was to biopsy the swollen lymph gland, he had consulted with the radiologist down the hall. There was no swollen lymph gland. There was nothing to biopsy. Apparently, the radiologist at the local hospital had mistaken a section of blood vessel where the dye had not penetrated for an enlarged lymph gland. What a relief! I could have jumped off the examining table and given him a big hug. He and his students examined my existing bump and talked to me briefly about my health.

About this same time, I had a session with a client of mine who also has cancer. He was aware of my cancer and gently challenged me to work with a complimentary approach to remove the bump. I consulted with my acupuncturist. Since there was no apparent hurry to remove it, we decided to try moxa. This is dried Chinese mugwort, which is formed into a tiny cone, placed on the point or area being treated, and lit with an incense stick. It burns slowly, moving the stuck energy by bringing heat and nourishment to the area, and is removed before burning the skin. My acupuncturist and another friend, who is also an acupuncturist, agreed to treat the bump with moxa three times a week. If the bump had been in a place where I could easily have reached easily, I could have done it myself. Well, within the course of a month's time, the skin began to change and the bump completely disappeared without a trace of a scar. I have removed two other bumps in this manner.

A number of years later, there continue to be no traces of the cancer, and my health is very good. The cancer in my bed was acknowledged, faced, felt, and the many lessons it offered learned. I continue my wellness program of good nutrition, exercise, and prayer. Acupuncture, craniosacral, and energy work, as well as massage, are regularly factored in when I feel the need for treatments. I hold strong to my belief that I am clear and beautiful from the inside out. I am very grateful for this experience, for it has taught me much and increased my compassion considerably for those who face this challenge.

The Guest House

This being human is a guest house.
Every morning a new arrival.

A joy, a depression, a meanness
some momentary awareness comes
as an unexpected visitor.

Welcome and entertain them all!
Even if they're a crowd of sorrows,
who violently sweep your house
empty of its furniture, still, treat each guest honorably.
He may be clearing you out
for some new delight.

The dark thought, the shame, the malice,
meet them at the door laughing,
and invite them in.

Be grateful for whoever comes,
because each has been sent
as a guide from beyond.

Rumi[18]

5. Tools for Acknowledging and Expressing Feelings

Here is a map to the territory of acknowledging and expressing feelings. Denying feelings or avoiding them only gives them power over us. We become victims. Recognizing our feelings gives us the opportunity to use the power they offer us. They are an expression of our humanness and the richness that is born of our experience. There are some specific steps that welcome the contributions that our feelings make to our health and well-being.

Acknowledging feelings is the first step. If you are having a hard time being in touch with your feelings, train yourself to pay attention to the experiences in your body with increased awareness. Take time to notice your feelings. Notice the tone of your voice, the actions you are making, your body language, and the sensations in your body. Talk about them with someone you trust.

---

[18] Colman Barks and John Moyne, trans., *The Essential Rumi* (New York: HarperSanFrancisco, 1995), p.109.

Write about them or draw them. The words or colors or shapes that you choose will help you describe your experience. Sometimes you can discover what you are feeling by simply describing what you are aware of, e.g., a body sensation or a picture in your mind. Give that sensation or picture a voice, as if it has a personality all of its own. Set up a dialogue between it and yourself, like in the previous example with the pain in my shoulder.

Paying attention to your dreams gives you clues about what is happening below your conscious level. Write them down immediately. Don't expect them to make logical sense. Play out or write out each part of the dream as if it were you. If you take the time to retell the dream from several of these parts, you may be surprised by the differences in the perspectives and learn more about yourself. Explore the feelings behind each part. For example, a house or piece of land in a dream may be as important as a person. Each has its perspective and reflects an aspect of you.

Acknowledging feelings helps you to discover what you are feeling and how you are experiencing them. There is no right or wrong to feelings. They are simply a part of what is present for you at any given moment. Acknowledging what you are feeling rather than running from them can make some of them less frightening.

If your feelings involve another person, **communicate openly and honestly**. If that doesn't feel possible, write him/her a letter. You can choose to send it or not. Sometimes the writing will be a big help in clarifying what you are really feeling. Maybe through several rewrites, you can move through the first layers of intensity and get the feelings down to communicable size or discover what is underneath, like the hurt that often rides under anger. Sorting through your feelings will probably allow you to express what you want to say to the other person in a way that he or she can hear you. If you want the other person to respond to you, you don't want to be intimidating or be so convoluted and garbled that the other person doesn't understand. You want to be clear and honest and put your words in a form that communicates the information that you wish to convey. Good communication is a very complex process.

Certain feelings may be uncomfortable or undesirable. Sometimes just by acknowledging your feelings, they begin to shift and change. In order to **release your feelings,** let them resonate through your body (feel them consciously) and feel them moving out of your body, dissipating in the atmosphere. Use images like a hot air balloon or waves in the ocean to move them away from you.

For example, imagine yourself standing in a clear beautiful river formed by many brooks coming down out of the mountains. The temperature of the water is very comfortable. You can see the ripples from the current moving around you. Hear the sweet sounds of the songbirds, or the call of the great blue heron overhead. Feel the current tug gently at your arms as you stretch them out and the smoothness of the round stones under your feet as you plant them firmly in the river bottom. As you stand there, you can imagine that the river runs right through you, as if it is gently and thoroughly washing out every cell in your being, including all of the spaces in-between. You might even be able to see a dark cloud of gunk being pulled out of your body, moving downstream, gradually being transformed by the water into clear liquid. Feel how it feels to be slowly and gradually cleansed of all the old fears and all of the old unwanted patterns of behavior that are no longer useful.

When the washing is complete, come slowly back onto shore. Be aware of the changes in your body, mind, and spirit. Remind yourself that you can choose to begin anew, with a fresh start. Let the warmth of the sun dry you and fill you with light, and let the earth underneath you hold you securely. Draw love down from the sun and up from the earth. Feel them filling your heart with hope and joy. Fresh and clean, you, too, now have something to give back.

Use prayer. "Let go, let God." Ask for help in letting go, receiving support, and feeling accompanied. You are not alone. Lift the veil from your eyes, feel the presence of God, a higher power, a divine essence, or the Great Spirit moving in your life. You may find yourself angry at God for giving you such a hard road to travel. Express that anger and work to let it go. Develop a relationship with God and feel God within you.

Maybe you have been feeling victimized by people or events in your life. You can choose to turn this feeling around by looking for the positive, the lessons, and the gifts that come from your experiences. Finding the gift empowers you to take charge and create a new reality for yourself.

A client remembered bitterly when her lover forced her to do something she hated. Finally, she stood up to him and said no. She had been very timid and remembers now how good it felt to finally be able to tell him no.

Feel empowered by being proactive rather than reactive. The very act of turning around and facing the monster (the fear or feeling) that has been chasing you is being proactive. Sometimes, looking the monster squarely in the eye brings it down to a manageable size. This monster may be an actual person, to whom you have given up your power, or it may be feelings about catastrophes that may or not be so real once you take the time to examine them.

Another client of mine worked for the sheriff's department. There were a series of events that had occurred within the department, as well as several work-related incidents that were very difficult for him. We discovered that when his integrity was challenged, he became very angry. At first, he wanted to believe that it was the department's fault that he was extremely anxious about going to work. It wasn't until he was willing to look at his anger that he could see that most of it came when he felt that they were questioning whether or not he had told the truth or had done what he was supposed to have done. Once he could acknowledge specifically what made him angry, then he could begin to change his reaction. He came to understand that sometimes people were accusing him of things just because he wore the uniform. He learned to sort out the things he could control from the things he could not. He began to see the administration of the department less idealistically. The anger dissipated quite quickly. In a difficult and challenging meeting with the sheriff, he heard my voice echo in his ear, "Don't give them your power." He was calm and in control because he felt his own power to make choices. He realized that he really could only control himself, and that he was the only one accountable for his integrity. He felt very good about himself as he took back the power that belonged to him.

Being proactive does not mean aggressively bowling over someone with whom you are having problems. Being assertively proactive means that you stand up for yourself in a way that is sensitive to others around you. By communicating effectively, the other person is able to hear what you want them to hear and neither of you feels disempowered in the process.

Develop a good sense of humor. Laughter can be enormously helpful in releasing feelings. Sometimes laughter may result from seeing fear as a cartoon character, like the Tasmanian Devil, who whirls himself into so many circles he doesn't know which end is up, or the Wicked Witch of the West, who is fearfully intimidating, but melts when doused with water. Another police officer I worked with came to see his tyrannical boss as Yosemite Sam. Instead of being paralyzed by this man's supervisory style, he saw Yosemite Sam instead of his boss. He could laugh inside and regain his own balance.

Cultivate the ability to laugh at yourself as a simple human who makes mistakes just like anyone else and sometimes looks pretty silly doing it.

Give yourself the opportunity to discover that you have family and friends who care. Being a martyr or stoic keeps you isolated and fearful. Take the risk of reaching out human to human and ask for help. Talk, share, laugh, and cry with others. Give and receive the love that is in you and available to you.

6. Shifting Feelings

We had had several beautiful, bright, clear, fall-like days in August, so I decided to spend the night sleeping out in the woods. I made myself a small fire and listened to the sounds as daytime animals and birds readied for the night and nighttime ones began to stir. After a day's work, it was very nice to lie on my back and gaze up at the bright lights peeking out though the leaves from the darkening sky. Several years ago, a tornado moved through my property, felling and trimming back a select number of trees. In this place, where I like to sleep, the top of a very large beech tree had been twisted off, opening a picture window to the northern sky. That tornado, which had happened while I was away visiting my sisters, opened up more light to my garden as well. What must have been a fearsome event resulted in a great gift. I was now among the trees and seeing some sky too.

I slept well with the companionship of my dog and several cats but was awakened sharply before daybreak with a disturbing dream. It was movielike, which is unusual for me. A man and woman had blown up a tall square building by putting explosives in the plumbing system. The building toppled onto its side, accompanied by some gunfire. That night, as the couple was making love, he was taunting her about what she had done.

I am not prone to violent dreams, and the clarity of this one was disturbing. Being wide awake, I decided to pray with my sacred pipe. I wasn't sure what I wanted, but in the course of the prayer, I asked to wrap the building, the man, the woman, and myself in loving presence. I had no idea what effect the prayer would carry. It felt right. I then remembered that I had heard a violent and painful story from a client the day before, so I wrapped her and all those involved, including the perpetrator, in love. The feelings shifted inside of me, so I was able to go back to sleep.

Later, I woke up to a very loud clucking. It sounded birdlike but seemed to be moving around on the ground. Whatever it was, it was big. I was able to walk quietly up to the top of the ravine to where I thought it might be. Luckily, my dog, who is usually right by my side, was still sleeping. The clucking started up again, and then like the shot of cannon, a huge iridescent purple bird flew through a ray of morning sunlight. It was a wild turkey. What an incredible sight to see!

According to Jamie Sams,[19] turkey reminds us to act and react on behalf of others. What we do, we do not for ourselves alone. Perhaps the turkey was an affirmation that giving away love was the best gift I could give. I was grateful for the rare treat of seeing the turkey and receiving his message. It was a fitting end to a difficult night.

The next night, at dusk, I had it in my head that I might find a turkey feather, since it was molting season. I took a pouch of tobacco to make an offering for the gift I was hoping to find. There was no bird feather, but on my way back to the campsite, I discovered that the huge yellow poplar tree that had come down several years ago was now covered with oyster mushrooms. I know this kind of mushroom well because I had been growing them from laboratory-produced mycelium the year before. Thanks were given for this gift.

When a friend phoned the day after my violent dream, she told me that several U.S. embassies in Africa had been bombed and that we had just retaliated by bombing Sudan and Afghanistan. This was very disturbing to me. It made me very sad that once again, we were responding aggressively, instead of out of a place of the heart.

When I retired for the night, I simply sat quietly for a long time. In my bag, I found a candle given to me by a dear friend. I lit it for peace, took out my gourd rattle, and began to shake it. A Lakota song, which honors the four

---

[19]   Jamie Sams and David Carson, *Medicine Cards: The Discovery of Power through the Ways of Animals* (New Mexico: Bear and Company, 1988).

directions,[20] came to mind. I danced, rattled, and sang around the candle for a
long time. I felt myself becoming light and more at peace. When the song came
to an end, I began the Balance Dance,[21] four sets in each direction. When words
came to mind, I spoke them out loud. Sometimes there were words and
sometimes silence. Nothing was planned. I was simply following what came to
mind to do next. As the prayer that I was making with my body, my words, and
my feelings emerged, it felt as if the whole forest was filled with a white light. I
asked that the column of light reach high into the sky and touch down into the
heart of the earth and that the beauty, love, and peace felt here resonate out to
wherever it was needed. I thanked the trees, plants, and animals for participating
with me in creating something that felt so beautiful.

By stopping to pay attention and taking the time to feel and respond to
inner impulses with a set intention, I was able to shift my feelings from the
disturbing to the peaceful.

This next story illustrates the way my experience changed when I began to
shift my perception from feeling like victim to feeling hopeful by understanding
that my difficult experience had a purpose. I was racing around, trying to finish
my list of tasks before I left for the West Coast to visit my sister. We were to be
sponsors for a beautiful teacher of ours in a Walk into the Grandmother Lodge
ceremony to be held the day before the summer solstice. My sister and I always
relish our time together and had planned a little vacation to the San Juan Islands
before heading to the ceremony in south central Washington.

One more task needed to be completed before I took my young puppy over
to friends for my time away. I had to feed one hive of bees. They seemed to be
the weakest of the three and had run out of sugar water. I wanted to be sure they
had enough before leaving for the week. It was much later in the day than I
usually go to them, but it was still light and warm, so I figured it would be all
right. One of the guard bees apparently had a different thought. I was struck
soundly on the cheek almost in the identical spot I had been stung a month ago.

I quickly put the jar in place, closed the hive, and ran back to the house.
I have had moderate allergic reactions before and didn't want one on the eve
of my trip. I had learned to scrape the stinger off. Pinching it off only shoots
more venom into the body. I had learned that the hard way. I took two Benadryl
and put a dollop of baking soda and water on my face, delivered my dog to
my friend's, and returned home to sleep a few hours before leaving for the
airport.

---

[20]   Each of the four directions: west, north, east, and south instruct us about an aspect
        of life that is essential to the whole of life. The specific teachings are discussed in
        a later chapter.

[21]   The Balance Dance is a movement meditation described in detail in the section
        on creating ritual.

The next day was spent cramped and feverish on a plane filled to maximum capacity. I felt as if I had a very bad case of the flu. When I arrived, my sister drove me to an acupuncturist. She said that I looked like I was holding a tennis ball in my cheek. I felt like I had been run over by a bulldozer. The last bee sting had been very successfully treated with three well-placed needles. This acupuncturist had a different approach. He put in what seemed like about fifty needles, taped ear tacks to my left ear, gave me the bee homeopathic cure, the naturopathic bee cure, and whatever other cure he could come up with. Unfortunately, I would have preferred simply the three needles. I appreciated his effort, but the overkill had no effect.

Late that afternoon, we caught our ferry to the beautiful San Juan Islands. Since I was still feeling very sick, the following day, I tried the Western approach. The doctor was very nice but said that there was nothing he could do for me. What a vacation! The first few days, I slept a lot. My loving sister played "Nurse Nancy," helping me navigate the path back and forth from our cabin to the bathrooms. I had lost my equilibrium. I wasn't eating and was having a hard time forcing liquid into my achy body. I worked with my medical assistance team, but there were no miracles there either. Most of the supplements that the naturopathic doctor had sold me were useless. I kept testing negative for them. My sweet sister helped so much more by snuggling close and reading to me a wonderful book of animal stories. We cried and laughed together.

Then the tide turned. I could no longer sleep. I was very restless and was plagued by headaches that gripped the base of my skull. It felt as if every cranial plate in my head was jammed. My head was going to explode at any moment. After about four days, I had a little energy, so we went only for a short walk out to a beautiful point overlooking the ocean. There were numerous interestingly shaped islands. Off in the far distance was a beautiful pastel column of rainbow light close to the horizon. I was cynical at first, thinking that it was caused by the exhaust coming from a ship I could barely see. A short while later, we walked around the inlet to a different viewpoint. Now the sun was lower on the horizon and the column of light had changed to intense rainbow hues. The column of light was not the exhaust from a ship but, apparently, some special atmospheric phenomenon. It was magnificent!

Seeing this column of light began a new train of thought. Just perhaps this illness was part of a higher purpose. Perhaps I was being inundated with a vast amount of energy that would take me to the next phase of development. I began to become aware of some worry I was harboring. I did not feel ready or capable for the work that I was being guided to do. What if this was part of the way I was being prepared? I was relieved to feel that once again I would get the help I needed when the time was right. This line of thinking seemed to check out with my medical assistance team.

An interesting thing began to happen as I began to think that there was a purpose in what I was going through. Immediately, the headaches began to dissipate; my energy picked up, and my feelings changed from heavy to light. I was hopeful again. I seemed to be clearly on the mend. And this trend continued.

Who really knows if my conclusion, that there was higher purpose in the bee sting and the flu like symptoms, was accurate? One of the difficulties I had had while I was so sick was that I couldn't focus long enough on any one healing image or relaxation exercise to help my situation. I was also feeling as if I were a victim of my sickness, as if I had no control or choices. I was also totally absorbed in the little drama that was happening to me. Definitely, the shift in my perceptions moved me out of a space where I felt victim to whatever was happening to me to a place where I had a sense of purpose. This impacted the course of my illness and that felt very powerful! The shift seemed to pull me out of the little picture into a much bigger one. Because it felt as if there was a reason beyond just me, I could begin to feel as if I were being prepared for the next step on my spiritual journey. This shift in my perception immediately initiated a healing process.

A few years ago, I was guided to do some "earth healing" work every morning at the pray-place. I would co-create a column of light with prayer, song, and sometimes dance. After about a year, I asked if I might get some feedback. Was what I was doing having any impact? The answer really took me by surprise. The Council of ADRON said, "You sound like a child, asking God to notice you." That was short and to the point. I hadn't thought that was my intention, but there was truth in their words. I decided from then on that my greatest feedback was the joy and love that I felt flowing through me. I still don't know whether the work I am doing has any effect beyond my own experience. I have decided it doesn't really matter. It feels right inside of me, and it brings harm to no one. My connection with nature helps me to work within the context of the whole picture to create balance and harmony.

As I teach clients to express and shift their feelings, I have found a metaphor that describes the process well. Imagine that you are a cellist and that you are also the cello. Each string has its own frequency and resonance, and each represents a feeling. If you are angry, one particular string is plucked. As it vibrates, it sends out a particular sound. If this anger is repressed, it is like placing your hand across the sounding board so that the sound is trapped inside the body of the cello. If the anger is expressed, the sound resonates outward through your instrument to the world around you. You can recognize it and express it effectively. Being willing to let go of the anger allows it to flow freely from your body. This way, there is no reservoir of past hurts or resentments built up to send you out of control. Each straw is manageably dealt with, so the camel's back is never broken.

One day, a young man came to me for spiritual counseling, not therapy. He had some issues he wanted to sort out. I agreed to sit with him. His fear was prominent. Apparently, he had spent much of his life carefully, critically analyzing himself and now found this way of being to be very painful. He felt that he had recently broken through into a different kind of experience. This new place was totally unknown to him. He felt very happy and nonjudgmental. As he became very focused on each step that he took, he realized that the present moment existed for him. There was no preformulated map to this new territory. This was very exciting because he felt so free. He felt unselfconscious in the flow with others around him.

While he was in this space, he spontaneously made a joke to his boss and was very surprised to hear a young woman nearby laugh. His fear came immediately to the foreground. He felt compelled to pull inward and hide in the old familiar criticisms. He felt like a rabbit caught in a snare. He had spent too much time admiring others and trying to be like them. They were so much better than ever he felt he could be. It was very hard to believe that he was good enough just as he was with all of his imperfections. The little joke that had come from somewhere inside of him was now clearly acceptable and even funny. How curious!

At one point during our conversation, he wanted to keep his focus inside while he was talking with me, so he kept his eyes closed. He didn't want to be distracted, because he saw me as the authority figure. He wanted to only to be in control himself. If he put up a shield all around himself and kept self-contained, perhaps he would be able to maintain himself and not be ruled by my thoughts and ideas. As he became aware of his sadness and his fear, he allowed them to resonate through his body. As these feelings dissipated, he released them and came back into contact with me. He discovered that he could interact, and he was able to maintain contact with himself at the same time.

I imagine that the next time he feels fear, he will practice letting go of his critical self-consciousness, he will trust in his process a little more and learn to love himself more fully.

This process is much like giving birth. The more we learn, the more fear we release. The more we get out of our own way, the more we allow the body to give birth to the child who knows the way naturally. We can work to get out of our own way and let our own birthing happen quite naturally with all of the love and support that are available to us.

7. Steps for Acknowledging and Expressing Feelings

1. **Acknowledge your feelings** by facing them.
2. **Take ownership and responsibility** for your feelings.
3. To express your feelings, **communicate them openly and honestly** in a way that is safe and in a way they can be heard.
4. To release them, **feel them**, allow them to **resonate throughout your body** and **feel them dissipate**.
5. **Use prayer**, talk to God about what you are feeling.
6. **Feel empowered by being proactive rather than reactive.**
7. **Develop a good sense of humor.**
8. Choose to look at the bigger picture. Why are these events happening to you now? When you can, **step back or fly above your situation and see if there is a larger, more meaningful pattern at work.**

CHAPTER IV

Healing

And the day came
When the risk to remain
Tight in a bud
Was more painful than
The risk it took to bloom . . .

Anais Nin

1. The Healing Journey

What happens when we move through a healing process?

We have the potential as human beings to be whole, healthy, in balance, and one with all things. We are capable of creating a harmonious flow between all parts of ourselves, which is, in turn, one with the harmonious flow of the divine universal energy. Our energy can be free to shift with the internal and external tides as we respond to our own experiences through the processes of adaptability and accommodation. At the same time, we can become intimately and consciously aware of these shifts and our connection to the greater whole.

At this point in our human evolutionary history, we are moving the seat of our consciousness from the mind to the heart. This does not mean that the mind gets left behind. It is far too valuable. When we shift our center to the heart, we are integrating the intelligence of the mind with the intelligence of our emotions. It is from this center that we also integrate our spiritual selves, for it is in the heart that we touch the Divine and can become the "I am." All of the metaphors we use of connecting with the earth and sky, God the Mother and God the Father, the Sacred Masculine and the Sacred Feminine, body and mind and gather these energies into the heart are addressing this integration. This becomes a way to bring heaven to earth, to be in unity, or to have Christ consciousness. Becoming one with all things happens by connecting these polar opposite concepts, integrating them, centering our experience on the energy of the heart, and connecting with the primordial field of awareness or God force that exists everywhere. Religious disciplines throughout the ages have given us a variety of methods to accomplish this state of being. We are closer than ever as a human spirit to experiencing this divine oneness. A journey that guides us toward healing our hearts and living our lives as prayers is one of the ways to bring us closer to our potential and to expand our levels of conscious awareness.

We are like a clear crystal cylinder that can be an open conduit for the loving energy that flows between God the Mother and God the Father. Instead, we have learned to tense up and to protect ourselves in many ways as we are buffeted by life's experiences. The crystal cylinder gets clogged up with gunk. Unresolved issues begin to interfere more and more with our ability to go with the flow, stay in the present moment, and be one with all things. As we begin a healing process, it is often a question of cleaning out the cylinder in order to recreate balance in our body, mind, and spirit, which are all part of our totality. That is why, if you are suffering from depression, it can be very helpful to work on your body and spirit as well as your mind. Imbalance reverberates throughout the whole being, as does healing.

The same is true for a disease of the body. Cancer is a good example. More and more cancer treatments include a journey into all of these areas: body/mind/spirit. We are not convenient little compartments, bodies separate from minds, which are in turn separate from our spirits. We can work to regain the natural balance and harmony that is an innate part of our system and move out into the world from the place of the heart and a peaceful inner world. This peaceful, loving, and compassionate energy becomes the gift we offer.

In healing, we are clearing away the layers of gunk and opening our hearts more and more to who we are and to the divinity that soars within us. Each of us has a unique expression that enriches the whole. When we live our lives as conscious prayers, it is as if we are a pebble tossed into a clear pond. The ripples move further and further out until the whole pond is undulating. The whole universe undulates in response to our energy, just as we are moved by the quality of energy emitted by the universe. Whatever energy we send out, the universe reflects back a similar energy. As we heal, so does the universe.

The following stories of L.W. and Christine are examples of two very powerful healing journeys. We can see in much more detail how each of these women chose to pursue an integration of body, mind, and spirit. L.W.'s journey began with a great deal of emotional distress and dissatisfaction with her ability to have a close, open, and loving relationship with her husband. Christine's journey began with an uninvited lump in her abdomen, which she discovered shortly after the birth of her son. Both of these journeys speak of the courage of these women to grab onto these difficulties and see them as opportunities from which to grow, learn more about themselves, and to become more whole and healthy human beings. Both took an active role in shaping their process.

2. L.W.'s Story

"I have reached a point now that it is hard for me to remember how bad I was or exactly when I started to get that way. I do remember calling my husband at work crying, 'When are you coming home? I'm losing it big time.' My only goal was to make it until he got home from work. Some days, making it would mean I wouldn't scream bloody murder at the kids, and other days, it meant that I could get out of bed and stop crying enough to take care of our children. Juney, our daughter, said one day, 'Why are you so sad all of the time, Mommy? Why are you always crying?' That was in the spring and summer of last year.

"I needed to do something, but I didn't know what. I had been to psychologists in the past and had been on antidepressant medication. I never really felt like those things had helped. Talk therapy was nice because it gave me a chance to get things off my shoulders. The medication helped me not cry incessantly, but it either made me into a zombie or so agitated that I felt like I was going to burst over the smallest infraction. I felt like the psychological and medical community had not been able to help me in the past. Why would they be able to help this time? I dragged my feet. I wanted to help myself, and I didn't even know where to start this time."

Through her work as a physical therapist, L.W. was learning about sensory integration and sensory defensiveness. "The more I learned, the more I felt like this was a big part of my problem," L.W. explained. "People with these problems have abnormally strong negative reactions to normally benign sensory input. These problems can be related to any of the senses: touch, hearing, vision, taste, and smell. Proprioceptive input (the ability to sense changes in the joints and muscles) and vestibular input (the ability to sense where you are in space) can also be affected. Negative reactions in these areas disrupt a person's capability to respond and interact with the world around them. According to Patricia Willbarger[22], OTR (occupational therapist), people with these problems can present with behaviors and symptoms such as anxiety, depression, controlling behavior, and strong emotional reactions to just about any kind of situation." L.W. learned to use a special kind of brush on her arms and legs. The brushing, when combined with joint exercises, helped to reset the part of the brain that processes sensory and emotional data. She was able to relax herself for about two hours, using this technique.

Earlier, when she had shared these thoughts with a psychologist she was seeing prior to coming to me, he expressed that he felt strongly that she was trying to avoid her real psychological issues. This analysis missed its mark. She

---

[22]   Patricia and Julie Wellbarger, *Sensory Defensiveness: A Comprehensive Treatment Approach* (CA: Avanti Educational Programs, 2001).

felt discounted and came to the conclusion that he did not understand the mind/body connection, which she was sure existed.

L.W. had started physical therapy with Mary focusing on a technique called craniosacral therapy. This was recommended as an adjunct to sensory integration treatment in one of the sensory defensiveness courses she was taking. "There were moments during physical therapy," she described, "when I was not sure if I could continue. The problem was not a physical pain, but the emotional upheaval that came during that work. After one extremely emotional physical-therapy treatment, it took me forty-five minutes before I could even think about trying to drive. It was several days after that particular treatment that I wrote, 'I will probably go insane or get better.' At that moment in time, I wasn't really sure which direction it would go." And yet she persevered with determination to find her way out of the darkness. "I felt like I should leave no stone unturned." L.W. came to see me when she was thirty-three. In our initial session, she described her experience as chaotic, highly emotional, as if she was always outside of herself. She went through nearly an entire box of tissues. "My heart feels like a void," she cried. "I feel like I continually put up walls between my husband. I deliberately hold him at bay, which does not allow any real intimacy between us. Lovemaking is out of the question because it is much too stimulating. I don't like him to touch me or kiss me." On the other hand, she expressed her desire to feel close to him, to be comfortably intimate with him. She also wanted to learn ways to calm down, instead of scattering and becoming very anxious.

Toward the end of the initial session, I moved my hands from the top of her head down the sides of her body several times about six inches from the surface of her skin as she was standing and then again off the body down her front and back. I was using my hands the way I had been taught by Mitek Werkus[23] to sense the quality of her energy. Her energy felt very scattered, as if it were buzzing on her sides, particularly on the left side of her head and in the front of her upper torso. It felt as if there was a huge block of energy about waist high through which it was difficult for my hands to pass. After I used my hands in this way, she reported feeling calmer and more centered. This was in the beginning of November.

During the next sessions, L.W. set an intention to bring joy and harmony to her mind and body. She and I worked on increasing her level of body awareness by focusing inward and reporting on her experience. I taught her several breathing exercises.

I felt that L.W. would be a good candidate for acupuncture and for healing-touch therapy. Both of these therapies work with the energy in the body.

---

[23] Mitek Werkus is a renowned energy healer, who was originally trained by Tibetan healers for the Catholic Church in Poland. He now practices and teaches in Bethesda, Maryland.

Acupuncture specifically works with points of energy along energy lines called meridians in the body that are associated with different organ systems. In five-element acupuncture, each of these organ systems is grouped into five elements: fire, earth, metal, water, and wood. Each of these also corresponds to a season and to a particular way of being in the world, psychologically and spiritually, as well as physically. It is a complex ancient Chinese healing system that uses the electrical interface (the acupuncture points) between the body and the etheric field surrounding the body to bring the body/mind/spirit back into a natural place of balance and harmony. I have found through my own personal use of acupuncture and from clients that acupuncture provides excellent support for the therapy process and seems to help people move through their "gunk" much more quickly. I felt, in L.W.'s case, that since she was overly sensitive to energy and having such difficulty managing her emotional dynamic that acupuncture would help her in very concrete ways to heighten her awareness of the subtleties of her own energy and bring her the balance she so badly needed.

Healing touch is also an energy-based form of treatment that works to align and balance the human energy field. The practitioner works off the body with his or her hands to promote the flow of subtle energy to areas of tension, trauma, and injury. The focus of treatment is to reactivate the body/mind/spirit connection, open the flow of energy in the chakras, and to eliminate areas of blockage to healing. Since I had palpated such huge energy blocks and imbalances in L.W.'s field, I felt that the healing touch approach would also be very valuable for her. Perhaps it would help her to consolidate her energy as well as facilitate a more even flow. With L.W.'s permission, I talked with each of these practitioners, after she had made appointments with them. I felt that a little heads up about her history and her hypersensitivity to energy would be useful. I also like to establish a connection with the other practitioners involved with my clients so that we can function as a treatment team to promote healing for the highest good of those we serve.

L.W. continued her story, "The acupuncturist, Penelope, asked me tons of questions about things I didn't even know were related. I started to see Tina for healing touch at the end of December 2001. Again, I told my story. Every time I had to tell the story, there was more to tell because of the discoveries I had made up to that point. I started to notice a pattern in some of the questions different people were asking me.

"Carol and Mary were both noticing that I was very sensitive energetically. I was feeling it, too. There were times when I just wanted to hide out in a cave and never come out. There were many times when I felt like I did not want to continue, and at the same time, I didn't want to get stuck in that horrible place. This is where Tina came in. I felt like we were sifting down through layers and layers. Some of the layers built on top of each other, and other layers were side by side. The different approaches fed off of each other and into each other. Some common themes kept coming up: staying grounded while I was expressing my emotions, maintaining a balanced energy field, and keeping my chakras open."

I introduced her to Machaelle Small Wright's medical assistance program and taught her how to do kinesiology (muscle testing). Flower essences, also a part of Wright's work, were available for addressing the health and well-being of the body/mind/spirit through the electrical system. These proved to be a helpful tool for her to calm her emotions, to feel more grounded, and to be appropriately connected to others without taking on their feelings. When she learned to use them on her own, they gave her a way to continue working in between sessions and gave her involvement with her healing process.

The question was raised concerning a history of sexual abuse. Her hypersensitivity to being touched, her difficulty with intimacy, and her highly emotional state were clues that perhaps sexual abuse had occurred in her past. Through the process of journaling, retrieving her own memories, and conversations with her mother, she began to piece together a possible explanation. Apparently, when she was an infant, a group of older women were often involved with her care. Probably all of them wanted to give her a lot of attention and passed her around among them, which greatly overstimulated this cute hypersensitive child. This well-intentioned affection was not sexual abuse, but because of her innate hypersensitivity to touch, these experiences were very overwhelming to a point of near intolerance.

L.W. came to understand that as a result of a lot of discontent in her household as she was growing up, she had internalized a lot of the turmoil. Because her mother's words and feelings often did not match, she was confused by the conflicting message. As a result, L.W. came to distrust her own feelings. One of the current ramifications of this experience was that she tended to easily absorb the emotions of her physical-therapy clients, as well as others who were around her. In the grocery store, for instance, she would get "flashes from others," which would contain information about them personally and emotionally. This was very disconcerting as well as exhausting and emotionally draining. We worked on helping her feel more protected in several ways.

Writing helped her to sort out her feelings from those of others. She also asked her medical assistance team for help. Learning to take control of her environment and her interactions came when she learned that she was able to step back from a situation to get the bigger picture. From this perspective, she could more easily be in touch with her own feelings and differentiate her them from others. She also learned she could say "no" when it was appropriate. This was centering and calming for her and added to the level of control, acceptance, and self-confidence she was beginning to feel in her life. We worked on self-esteem, using self-concept exercises, to learn more about how she described and felt about herself.

"January and February brought more work in all the areas," L.W. reported. "As I worked through the more superficial issues, I felt like I had to get the base of the pyramid straight. If the base was not right, then all the hard work up to this point would be wasted. A common theme having to do with my heart came up in February. Healing touch, work at Carol's, and acupuncture all dealt with my heart. Again, I could feel all the different modalities working together to support me as I went through changes."

She brought her husband in for several sessions during this time. They had been fighting a lot, and both recognized that she had erected a barrier of sadness and anger between them. They both wanted more intimacy. She had been badly wounded in her first major relationship, which was continuing to impact her marriage. We focused on active listening and self-awareness skills, and they learned to connect with each other's energy through a series of exercises.

After a short period of openness, she erected the barrier again as fear of the new and unknown became strong. As this work progressed, they learned to give each other positive feedback. When she took the risk to open her heart again, she began to experience herself as much more grounded and focused. As she became aware of her feelings and trusted herself and her husband more, she was able to manage her occasional upsets successfully within appropriate limits and was able to move with ease through the details of the day. Her husband was very supportive of her self-care, which consisted of writing, reading, and painting with watercolors. During this time, their level of intimacy gradually increased.

L.W. decided that she was ready to try friendships with women, which had always been hard for her. I suggested that she come to the Sacred Women's Retreat that I was coleading with my sister, Starfeather. Here, she would have the opportunity in a safe environment to experiment with connecting with others. At this intense weekend, she managed her feelings well and learned to open up to others. The process of making friends is continuing to grow in a satisfying direction.

Shortly after the weekend, she had an energy drawing by Starfeather, which showed three additional energy fields connected to her heart with threads of energy. "This was not something that entirely made sense to me," L.W. reported, "but I decided to trust that everything that had been recommended to me so far had been helpful. If I was going to truly leave no stone unturned, I needed to follow up with Starfeather's recommendation. Next week, I went to Carol's, unsure of what I was embarking upon. I left two hours later with one more of my many stones turned over."

In this session of relaxed heightened awareness, she was able to disconnect from these energy fields after understanding that they had come initially in an effort to protect her. She was comfortable experimenting with them "hanging out in the neighborhood," while she experienced what life would be like without their continual input. The end result of their desire to protect her had been very confusing, because they, in turn, overloaded her with their own sensory input. As they disentangled their energy fibers from her heart, she felt much more expanded and spacious. She described her experience as if the "closets in her brain had been cleared out and were empty."

Four days of doing very well followed this session; then she felt extremely overwhelmed. She worked with Tina, her healing-touch practitioner, to consolidate her energy again. I learned that I could have perhaps helped her be less vulnerable after such a powerful session with flower essences and a process of sealing her energy.

For two months after disconnecting from the three fields of energy and her work with Tina, she experienced feeling good and clear. Because L.W. still felt like she was holding back from her husband in a way that was dissatisfying to them both, she decided to experiment one night. She imagined a chalice filled with her "essence," which she wanted to share with him. As she poured it into her sleeping husband, she became very upset and couldn't calm herself down. When they came to their session, I had them focus with their eyes closed on self-awareness using a humming breath. I suggested that they stretch their hands out toward one another and experience the energy passing between them. Taking turns, I asked each one of them to use their hands to sense the energy in the other's body by keeping their hands off the surface of the body. When L.W.'s husband was using his hands to sense her energy, I had her control his motion by telling him to stop and start only when she was comfortable. We decided to schedule an individual appointment to explore the difficulties that were still present.

At this point, it seemed to me that it might be worthwhile exploring if there was any emotional carryover from a past life. Sometimes, when there have been difficult issues, the soul brings emotionally charged material forward into the next life, giving an opportunity to bring resolution and healing. L.W. was having such difficulty creating intimacy with her husband. She would freeze up in a way that seemed more than what was warranted by her current life experience. It was just a hunch on my part. I have been trained in past life therapy by Roger Woolger[24] to recognize symptoms that might be important to explore in this way. In the previous session with her husband, she had talked about feeling as if her heart was being grabbed. He certainly was not grabbing her heart, literally or figuratively. What did that mean? I was curious.

During this next session, she went easily into a deep state of relaxation and took the time to revisit the energy fields that had been previously released and who were still in the "neighborhood." She expressed her gratitude to them for the protection they had tried to provide. Then she went back to a memory of a past life by using this sensation at her heart.

Once again, she felt as if something was grabbing it, which she was able to identify as fear. As she focused on this sensation, she found herself in a very small space, terrified. It evolved that she was a black slave hiding in a bid for

---

24   Roger Woolger, *Other Lives, Other Selves: A Jungian Psychotherapist Discovers Past Lives* (New York: Doubleday, 1987).

freedom and better circumstances for his wife and child. He was caught, caged, and sold. His life became filled with hard work and drunken brawls. During one of these fights, he had killed another man whose death had not come immediately. As he died slowly, the man had suffered greatly. Because he (L.W.) had killed another man and had been unable to put him out of his misery, he experienced a tremendous pain around his heart.

When he was forty years old, after years of pain and guilt, he died in a fight. At this point of death, he was able to see that his son and wife had lived a happy life and were freed after the Civil War. L.W. worked on forgiving herself. After this regression experience and her new understanding, she was able to communicate much more openly with her husband and developed a more deeply loving and intimate relationship with him.

Over an ten-month course of therapy, L.W. had changed dramatically from a woman who would cry nonstop during her sessions, a woman, who was scattered and unfocused and who could not tolerate lovemaking with her husband because it was so overwhelming, who was constantly stressed emotionally and physically because she was taking on the emotions and pain from her clients and those around her, to a woman who is confident and strong, centered, focused, and loving with friends and intimate with her husband. She worked hard over this period within using the treatment modalities of sensory-integration therapy, psychotherapy, craniosacral therapy, healing touch, and acupuncture. She continues to grow as she learns to balance her time with her two children, her husband, work, and friends. She has decided to develop a specialty of working with children and adults who have sensory-integration problems. She is realizing her intention to bring joy and harmony to her mind and body.

"I continued to see Penelope, Tina, and Carol, uncovering deeper and deeper layers of myself that I had not previously understood. I felt like I had finally found the key to what I needed to help myself. It wasn't just one person who could help me; it was a whole group. All the parts of the puzzle were important for me: the sensory-integration therapy, the craniosacral treatment, the acupuncture treatment, the healing-touch treatment, and the psychology/talk therapy aspect. I feel like I truly have turned over every stone that was presented to me and have reaped the rewards for the work we have done.

"There are times when I still struggle with old patterns of behavior, but the difference is that I have new strategies to help me regain control. I have learned to help myself."

3. Christine's Story

"I'm rapidly approaching my one-year mark since my last surgery," Christine begins. "In a few short months, I will have to decide whether or not to continue taking the chemotherapy that I've been on since December of 2001. It has been a time of introspection for me, thinking of where I am, where I've been, where I want to go. I've learned so much in such a short time and still have so much more to learn.

"My adventures started soon after the birth of my son Ethan. He was born via an emergency cesarean section in May of 2000. Several days after returning home, I noticed a lump in my abdomen. Assuming that it had something to do with my recent surgery, I went back to the OB and joked that he had left his Rolex inside. Several noninvasive tests were performed. I saw a gastro-intestinal specialist and a general surgeon. I was having no symptoms, no discomfort, and the tests were inconclusive. Perhaps it was a hematoma (something like a bruise) from the trauma of the surgery, so we decided to wait a month or two and see if it dissipated on its own."

Four months after the birth of her son, Christine was diagnosed with colon cancer at the age of twenty-three. The tumor was removed surgically August 8, 2000, and she was put on a difficult course of chemotherapy. She describes her experience as follows:

"I underwent surgery at the hands of a wonderful, compassionate, and talented surgeon. She and my family were worried about my health, while I was worried about continuing my breastfeeding relationship with my three-month-old son. I was scared of getting poked with needles, too. The seriousness of what I was about to undertake was lost on me. I don't think I was in denial, I don't know. I just had a really skewed perspective.

"The surgery was long but successful. The doctor reported the success to my waiting family with tears of relief in her eyes. I woke up in more pain than I had ever imagined possible. I hadn't considered that it was going to be too much worse than my C-section. I'm so glad that I had no clue; otherwise I would have been too scared going into it.

"The surgery included removing the damaged portion of my colon, a portion of my small intestine that the tumor had adhered to, and a portion of my stomach that was also touching the tumor. The tumor was removed as well, along with as much of the surrounding mesentery as possible, including around twenty-one lymph nodes.

"We were soon informed that the tumor was cancerous. It was very large, about the size of a grapefruit. The surrounding lymph nodes were clean, but there were some tumor cells found in one of the lymphatic channels. The doctors were not sure if they were actually traveling somewhere, or if they had been dislodged during the manipulation of the tumor during surgery. Either way, their presence wasn't good news, so chemotherapy was suggested.

"I stayed in the hospital for just over a week, during which time the doctors and anesthesiologists worked with me to choose a pain medication that wouldn't hinder nursing my infant son. My family was incredible, bringing him to me first thing in the morning and not leaving with him until late at night. Still, I missed Ethan terribly during the hours that we were apart. I pumped milk throughout the night, fearful of losing my supply. My husband or my father stayed with me every night.

"When I came home, I stayed with my parents so that I had help 24/7, while my husband was at work. I was still in pretty rough shape. I remember not being able to sit or stand upright, feeling like they sewed me up too tightly or something. I could only eat several bites of food before my stomach would be painfully full.

"I was given a month to heal. Then I started my chemotherapy treatments. Of course, I had to wean my son. I can say, without a doubt, that that was the most painful part of the whole diagnosis. I had planned on nursing him until he was ready to stop. I had imagined a long, fulfilling, close nursing relationship with him. Instead, I had to deny my tiny infant son my breast that he had known up to this point as a source of nourishment, comfort, security, and love. I had to turn him away when he would nuzzle me through my shirt and gently guide his little hands away as they pulled at my clothing. Fortunately, he adjusted more smoothly than I did.

"The standard chemotherapy treatment for colon cancer, at that time, was a drug called 5FU. Around the time of my diagnosis, however, they were experimenting with using another stronger colon-cancer drug called—(ugh, can't believe I don't remember the name!). This drug had traditionally been used for patients suffering from recurrences. The idea was that if it was more effective at treating recurrences, perhaps it would also be effective at preventing them. So we chose to combine the medications in hopes of coming at it from all angles. I had chemo once a week, four weeks in a row, then one week off. The— made me really sick. The day of my chemo was really rough. I was horribly nauseous and vomited pretty much all day long. I would usually wake up the next morning feeling worn out but pretty much back to normal. I was grateful that it was only one day out of seven that I was sick. We experimented with different antinausea drugs. Finally, we tried Marinol, which was really effective at first but slowly tapered off. Fortunately, I was almost done with the regimen before it became completely useless to me.

"As a family, we muddled through the six months of chemotherapy. Living it, it didn't seem so difficult. It just *was*. Looking back at it now, I wonder how we survived. Kevin, my husband, was a gem, and my son was the greatest gift of all. When you have a small child, you don't have the luxury of sitting up in bed each morning wondering, 'How do I feel?' You just get up and do what needs to be done. It's not optional. I think that Ethan prevented me from overanalyzing the situation and threw me headfirst into survival mode. It wasn't until March when it was over and we had a taste of 'normality' again that we realized how intense it had been."

When I first saw Christine on January 3, 2001, she described her situation as follows: "I was a college kid who didn't eat well, drank too much, and didn't take care of herself. Now, it really matters." She had stopped smoking, had started to eat well, and cared a great deal about the health of the child. Having had to stop breastfeeding made her sad, and she wondered if she could re-lactate when the chemo was over. She was interested in seeking alternative health care and also wanted to understand how she could stay healthy. Christine did not feel that her extended family was supportive of her choices in parenting or in her choices for health care. She had a strong desire to learn to be the best parent she could be. She wanted to have more children, but it was not yet clear if her fertility had been compromised by the surgery and the chemotherapy. Her husband was an active participant as a father. He was very busy at work and in his electrical engineering masters program. She also had questions about her spirituality. She had been brought up Catholic and had become dissatisfied with some of the doctrines.

Over the course of her therapy, she was searching for answers to some big questions: "As a mother, am I making the healthiest choices for my child? What can I understand about my illness and how has it functioned in my life so that I can do things differently? How can I take good care of myself and become healthier? How can I get support outside of my extended family for the new ideas that I want to try as a parent and in search of health and well-being? How can I become more independent from my extended family? What spiritual path suits me best?"

Over time, I made several referrals and suggestions. She began acupuncture treatment, started a yoga class, began work with a healing-touch practitioner and had several consultations with Starfeather. She also explored the work of Machaelle Small Wright by setting up a medical assistance program team and occasionally took flower essences. She did a lot of research concerning nutrition for both herself and her son, decided to eat organically, and experimented with a yeast-free diet. To expand her spiritual practice, Christine started to go to Unitarian Universalist services and attend classes in Native American philosophy and spirituality. With all of this work, it was imperative that she pay close attention to that which had integrity with her own beliefs, goals, and intentions.

Christine was not very aware of her body/mind/spirit, so she began to learn how to pay detailed attention to her inner life. I taught her several breathing techniques geared to increase her ability to relax and focus, as well as feel her emotions and physical form. These were the precursors to some meditation techniques, which she later learned.

"One of the things that has always seemed so strange to me was that I had no clue that something so *wrong* was going on inside of me," Christine reflected. "I never had any symptoms. I felt fine. I had no inner voice whispering to me to pay attention. That was and still is really disturbing to me. Carol and I talked about and practiced ways to reconnect with my physical body, to develop mindfulness, to develop and to trust my intuition. We talked about alternative therapies that might be helpful to me. Carol helped me realize the importance of a body/mind/spirit approach. I took a class she offered that taught on meditation. I began a deeper exploration of my spirituality and tried acupuncture.

I found a way to embrace and incorporate some of these things into my daily life." In addition, she worked with the principles of setting an intention. She cleverly put her altar on a tray so that she could set it out of the reach of her very active son while he was awake, bringing it down when she had time to focus her attention on it.

We worked on identifying negative patterns of behavior. She had an adversarial relationship with her mother, whom she felt pushed "all her buttons" and then would get hurt when Christine responded defensively. She began to experiment with new ways to set loving limits: "Let's not go there right now." We reframed the "little crazy" label she had been given by her family to "wonderfully creative." She made efforts to act more independently from her family and give herself the positive support she needed.

Her husband was very supportive. Christine was pushing to move away from her family in an effort to become more independent, but her husband requested that he be able to finish his masters program first. She agreed, understanding that it was as important to practice the conscious-living lifestyle she wanted here as well as elsewhere.

She was making good gains in treatment, but her story continued: "A port had been put in place to facilitate the chemotherapy after my veins collapsed. In early October, seven months after chemo had stopped, the port was removed. I was a little tender the next day but forgot it quickly when my son incurred a minor injury that absorbed all of my worry and concern. I didn't even think about my tender collarbone.

"About a week and half post surgery, I went back to my surgeon to get the stitches removed. She happened to ask, offhandedly, when my last blood tests were. It was time for them, so she sent me down to the lab for my blood to be drawn.

"The next day, I had a call from her, but she didn't leave a message. Fear and worry began to seep into my heart and mind. My stomach tightened, and I worried when I returned her call. She wasn't available and would return my call. I was very anxiously waiting. When the phone rang, she asked if I have someone home with me. I knew that this was not a good sign. I told her that I didn't. I was alone with Ethan."

"'Your tumor markers are fairly substantially elevated,' she reported.

"I tried hard not to cry. The whole next week, I felt pretty numb and scared. My family was fearful and worried too. We were referred to a surgical oncologist at Washington Hospital Center. He was supposed to be 'the best of the best.' I took him my scans and the news was not good. The tumor was in my abdomen and parts of my other organs seemed to be involved. But the biggest concern was that the tumor seemed to be working itself around my aorta. There was no way to predict how the surgery would go. The doctor wouldn't know until he had my belly open if he could remove the tumor without harming my artery.

"I called Carol immediately, and we fell into action, forming a team of healers to support me though this trial. She was one of the first people I told about my elevated tumor levels. Carol arranged to see me as soon as she could, and she helped me with my fear, worry, and anxiety. Then she gave me the name of a healing-touch practitioner and an acupuncturist that she thought would be helpful to me in preparing and working through what lay ahead.

"Carol and I continued to meet. She helped me with practical things such as nutritional things that I could do to strengthen my immune system and strengthen my body. She held me and let me cry. We walked in the woods, talking about death, dying, and the unknowns. She held me again and let me cry some more. She helped me develop and work with my MAP team as another source of support. My family was wonderful support as well, but having a confidante that was more removed from the situation was a huge relief."

During those days, she reported not being afraid of dying but didn't want to go now because her son was young and needed her. She was most afraid that he would grow up and not know how much she loved him or that he might possibly not even remember her. I encouraged her to write him a letter, which he could read when he was older. We went for a long walk in the woods, going over the long list of questions she wanted to ask her surgeon. She also wanted to bring some healing music into surgery with her as well as request some healing-touch work while she was in the hospital.

When she went home, she and her husband had a long honest conversation about all of the "what ifs." She and Kevin made out wills and decided who would have custody of their son if anything should happen to both of them. This helped her feel much better.

Later, we did some preparation for the surgery, which consisted of visualization. She found a quiet, peaceful, and healing place on the earth, which she described as a moss-covered clearing in the forest where she could look up at a patch of blue sky through the green leaves. This gave her much comfort. She was to use this image when she began to feel anxious. We also worked on the image of the Medicine Buddha over her head, holding her medicine in his hands. She could feel the lines of love and healing energy and light extending into her body. We expanded her medical assistance team to include those who would serve her well during surgery.

"A few weeks prior to my surgery, I met with the acupuncturist. Our initial consultation was pretty intense as I recounted for her my journey to that point. Penelope was so open and so sincere; it was easy to confide in her. I trusted her immediately. We did both needles and energy work, supporting my physical body through this stress, as well as my spiritual and emotional well-being.

"Tina, the healing-touch practitioner, and I had actually met prior to my asking her to join my team of healers. We didn't realize it initially, but she had massaged me after the birth of my son, which had been one of the hospital's "perks" for new mothers. Tina had stood in the doorway of my hospital room, looking like an angel, tall, with a halo of light hair and her sweet energy shining from within her. She asked me if I would like a massage. Her touch was wonderful, and I think I dozed off to sleep either toward the end or soon after. Upon awakening, I truly wasn't sure if it had only been a dream. My husband confirmed that it had actually happened. I suspect he was a bit envious, too.

"In any case, upon meeting Tina for my consultation, I remembered her immediately. Tina has such a wonderfully broad background in both complementary therapies and conventional medicine, providing a new bridge between the two. In the few weeks before my surgery, she worked with me, teaching me affirmations about my body, as well as working with my immune system and other body systems, so I could be as strong as possible going into surgery. She also loaned me a really wonderful book that was incredibly helpful in my surgery preparation (*Prepare for Surgery, Heal Faster,* by Peggy Huddleston).

"Having these three amazing women on my side was so empowering. It gave me much confidence and comfort. I had three sets of knowledgeable and caring ears, as well as their other numerous talents and gifts to support me. With their guidance, I created a game plan for going into this challenge of a lifetime.

"Every day, presurgery, I devoted time to prayer, relaxation, and meditation. I used various relaxation techniques that Carol had shared with me and then concentrated on visualizing my body being 'soft and warm and full of light.' I imagined being surrounded by a warm glow of protective and strengthening light. I imagined being with my family in years to come, watching my son turn two, three, ten, and so on. I imagined my surgeon opening my stomach up to find only dazzling light, no cancer to be seen (reach high, right?). I imagined waking up from surgery to be told that I was whole and healthy. I imagined my incision and any internal 'stuff' (since I wasn't sure exactly what was going to happen) healing quickly and comfortably.

"My surgery was scheduled for the end of October. That day, I donned headphones to drown out the clinical conversation that occurs in the course of surgery. Even when unconscious, the mind registers sound, and I didn't want anything negative getting through. When meeting with the anesthesiologist presurgery, I asked her if she would read from a list of affirmations for me, both as I was becoming unconscious and as the surgery was wrapping up. The affirmations included things like, "Your surgery has gone very well." "Your—will heal quickly and comfortably." "You will awaken and feel comfortable." I asked her to improvise as she saw appropriate as the surgery unfolded and she knew more details of what went on. I also called on my MAP team to be with me, inviting any deva I could possibly think of, as well as my higher self, and the higher selves of everyone in the OR with me (the surgeon, the anesthesiologists, the nurses, the student doctors, etc.). And of course, I prayed.

"On the day of surgery, I was scared. Things happened very quickly. My emotions felt too big. My husband was there with me, and I could see his fear and concern, too. But I knew I had done everything I could to prepare myself, and I just had to let go and have faith. I knew I had literally dozens of people praying for me. I was in good hands."

The surgery was very long and very difficult. Apparently, the tumor was wrapped around her aorta. The surgeon had worked long and hard to remove it. Just when he thought he would have to give up, the tumor became free, and he was able to remove it entirely.

"I woke up early the next morning [my surgery had started around noon the day before]." Christine continues, "I was hooked up to a respirator and had a huge tube shoved down my throat. My throat hurt, and when I tried to breathe on my own, I couldn't. There was a moment of the worst panic that I ever remember experiencing. I felt as if I was suffocating. Finally, I realized that I had to try not to breathe for the breathing tube to work. It was horribly uncomfortable, my whole body hurt, and I was very scared. There was a nice nurse right beside me who tried to calm and comfort me. I eventually fell back asleep and woke again to the same panic. This time, I wondered how the surgery went. Was it successful? I knew that I hurt so badly, that I wasn't just opened up and sewn right back up. I guessed that he had to have done some sort of work inside of me. Again, I was calmed by the nurse. I couldn't talk through the tube, which was also very frustrating.

"The next time I woke, a man came to try to get me to cough (was he crazy?) to see if he could remove the tube. Somehow, he determined that it wasn't time yet. I remember crying and shaking my head back and forth and trying to plead with him with my eyes.

"Finally, I awoke again; they removed the tube, and my parents were allowed to see me. My husband had gone home after the final report of the surgery to be with our son, as we had planned. I was so relieved to see my parents. The look of relief and concern combined in their eyes as they looked at me made my heart swell. I tried to talk, but no noise would come out of my throat. I managed to mouth/rasp 'How did it go?' to them. They told me the good news that the doctor was able to remove all of the tumor.

"Later, I learned the details. They had to disturb my pancreas, which is apparently a very sensitive organ. 'It doesn't even like to be looked at,' the doctors had said. Due to that, they anticipated an even longer period of healing for me. Initially, they had quoted three to four weeks, but they were expecting to add possibly another two weeks to the original time."

Her recovery astounded the medical staff. I paid two visits. One was soon after the surgery and one a week later. It was amazing to see the difference in her the second time. She was so full of life and vitality. She was up and about playing with her son, smiling and full of energy. They released her in record time, only thirteen days.

"Post surgery, I continued with my daily devotion to prayers, relaxation, visualization, and affirmations. I called upon my MAP team regularly. Whenever I had a few moments to myself, I would take the time to ground myself and quiet my mind and mentally pamper my body. I would imagine an organ or what-have-you, and imagine it bathed in warm, golden, healing light. I mentally talked to it and stroked it. It sounds silly writing it all out, but something worked! I continued to use these techniques as I dealt with pain, with the occasional bouts with nausea, with having to have my IV reinserted, as well as when the various tubes in me were removed.

"My healing team continued to support me. Carol visited me several times, bringing sweet and thoughtful gifts in addition to the comfort and warmth of her presence. Penelope came several times and helped me with energy work, and Tina was available via phone and held a remote healing for me."

When Christine was back home, we took the time to examine the possible origin of her disease from a psychological perspective. She came to the conclusion that for most of her life, she was constantly being overwhelmed by the amount of "stuff" that she received from her parents. Her father had grown up very poor and had had very little. "To say no to them is to fly in the face of their generosity, and they ended up hurt." Over and over, she would ask for something simple that took thought and time, e.g., "Make me a photo album of the family and tell me about the aunts whom I don't know." They never seemed to understand and were now bombarding her son with all of the fifty million toys that he could ever want.

Her analysis made sense in that it is the colon's job to sort out what is important nourishment for the body to keep and what is to be discarded because it has no value for the health of the body. The metaphor was pretty transparent. Her challenge continues to be to deal with the "things" she is given gracefully and sort through what is useful and what is not.

She was upset because the recurrence of the disease and the surgery made her dependent again instead of fostering the independence she prized so highly. She simply learned that she needed to accept her parents for all of who they are and be very grateful for their help and support. She learned to claim her independence in small areas at first, as she could manage them.

It was recommended that she do chemotherapy again. The last course of treatment had been so debilitating and unpleasant that she was fearful of what the "poison" would do to her body this time. Once again, we used visualization. She traced the roots and lines of light of the medicine that was to be given to her, and she was able to connect with the positive intention behind it. She saw herself place the medicine on an altar to the earth. The earth infused her body with healing energy, preparing Christine for her turn to give back the many lessons she has learned. We spent some time exploring what this giveaway of herself might mean. Since she can't get pregnant at this time, she has chosen to nurture the creative spirit within her and see where it leads.

In reviewing her healing journey, she spoke, "I believe that the team approach was paramount to my successful surgery and recovery. Each member of my team brought their own education, experience, talents, and gifts. This is truly a case where they worked synergistically and 'the sum is greater than the whole.' I know that the support I received from one member of my team enhanced the work of the other, and so on.

"I have learned so much and look forward to learning more. I have such a heightened appreciation for everything in my life and for my life itself. Each day is truly a gift. I am so grateful to be given this perspective. There is still fear and uncertainty. But hope and faith outweigh it by far."

Tina reported that "Christine continued to come for maintenance and support treatment now on a monthly visit schedule. She incorporated meditation, honoring intention, and setting time for self-care. She has shown an eagerness to learn more about herself as she started yoga and sought counsel from Starfeather. She was able to create a sacred medicine box for her chemotherapy pills and set aside time for her body to rest with sacred naps as she integrated the healing support that she had set up for herself. She has been responding well to her chemotherapy, adjusting to the changes in her body with the chemo. She has a positive outlook for herself and her family as they build a new home. She has taught me a lesson in the courage of the human spirit and the amazing results of her calling together her team of supporters for her cancer journey. The key was that she became an active participant in her healing, maintained a positive attitude, and drew a team of healers together to help her navigate some very difficult and challenging waters."

4. The Cycle of Change

Can we change aspects of ourselves that we may no longer be content with? This is a question I am often asked: "Can I really change?" Yes, and we have to be willing to choose to change. Rather than thinking that we have to remove parts of ourselves, we might begin to imagine that we can add new ways of being and responding. By expanding our repertoire of behavior, attitudes, and experiences, we can add more possible responses. Here is an example.

The young man, of whom I spoke earlier, was very practiced with analyzing his every move. He wanted to grow spiritually and find some easier and freer ways of being. Having discovered happiness, he wanted to be free to explore this new way of being. How could he embody happiness without always having to retreat into the old familiar patterns of fear and self-doubt? Those fears were not going to disappear so quickly. In a certain sense, they served as old friends. Now they helped him grow and change in a different way. He learned to be an excellent observer of himself. His new challenge was to learn to experience himself without criticism. His fears may have protected him against the harsh criticisms of others. Perhaps he could learn to use those fears as a red flag signaling him to move inside to the place of his own inner authority. What if he chose not to give his power away to others? Experimenting with a myriad of new ways of being could lead him to the ones that best suit his needs.

The cycle of change goes something like this: becoming aware of ways that we think, feel, or behave that no longer meet our needs or desires leads to dissatisfaction. L.W. became painfully aware of the lack of intimacy in her marriage. What had been acceptable before was no longer tolerable. Christine had cancer but could only begin to seek a cure when she discovered the lump in her abdomen and became very worried about it.

Acknowledging the difficulty, the pain, or the problem helps us to pay attention and to feel it more consciously. As we open to the experience of these feelings, we become more familiar with them when these feelings arise. As we become present to our pain and dissatisfaction, our experiences become more intense. Old patterns become glaringly apparent. This intensity often serves as motivation to do something about it.

If we can work to feel them fully with no sense of judgment or criticism, we can come to understand how these behaviors, these symptoms, have functioned for us. We can begin to get the help we need. Both L.W.and Christine chose to seek a variety of healing methods and found that a team approach gave them good support and different points of view that were each helpful.

Beginning to experiment with new solutions to old problems sometimes feels like we are about to jump off the edge of a cliff. We are choosing to leave the old familiar territory. It is not as if we are doing surgery on a part of our psyche and removing it, but we are choosing to experiment with and expand ways that we respond. Some of these experiments may be successful, and some may be unsatisfactory. It takes a lot of energy and conscious awareness to try something new.

The decision to change comes from within. No outside authority can dictate our willingness to change. There is no magic wand, and there are lots of wonderful ways to take this journey.

Here are some ways to experiment. Become a careful nonjudgmental observer of others. Is there someone you admire who behaves differently than you do? What if you were to try on a new way of doing things, similar to what you see in the other person? Don't copy the pattern of behavior exactly, but make the new behavior a version that fits for you. Look for successful behavior in others and try it on for size. Once, I was helping a police officer quit smoking. He smoked four packs a day and almost every gesture he made with his hands involved cigarettes. What was he going to do with his hands now that he was choosing not to smoke? I suggested he observed what others did with their hands and try out some new gestures. He actually found the transition much easier than he imagined and was able to put the cigarettes away for good.

There is the familiar saying, "Fake it until you make it." Take time to picture in your mind's eye the new behavior you want to incorporate into your repertoire. This way, you can run through a number of possibilities to find the one that feels closest to what you want for yourself. See yourself in a new way.

What if you were to take the time to slow down, sit, and meditate? Practice by paying attention to the inside of your own experience. Breathe in divine grace and let go of cares and tensions as you breathe out. Feel the floor underneath you and the earth beneath that. Be aware of the ceiling above and the sky high above that. Tune into your heart and breathe. Reach out into the space in front of your heart and behind it. Connect with the teachers both big and small in your life. Ask for help if you need it and take the time to listen to the response.

Love yourself.

Make a pact with yourself that your words and actions will match. Practice being assertive, by saying what you think. Do this in a way that others around you, including you, can hear what you have to say. Stay in the present with your thoughts and feelings. See what emerges.

Journal or paint or dance or sing or drum early in the morning before the sun rises and everybody else is asleep.

Consult with practitioners in a variety of healing modalities. Find out which ones may be particularly suited to your problems.

Place a written affirmation on your bathroom mirror. Every morning and night, when you are looking into the mirror say, "I have value as a human being." Or whatever you are working on believing about yourself. You need to believe in yourself before others will believe in you. Learn to receive as well as give and vise versa. Listen to what others say about you. When you receive a compliment and accept it by simply saying, "Thank you!" Maybe add that to your mirror collection. Begin to believe in yourself.

Imagine that you are standing in back of your house, at the edge of the woods. There is the well-worn path that you always take when you go for a walk. It is very familiar territory, but it takes you in a direction that you no longer want to go. So one day you decide to go exploring, to go off the beaten path, in order to discover something new. Going a new way could mean you might get lost, so you gather up your courage. A small opening through the trees catches your eye. As you walk along, ducking under low branches, you see a hardly perceptible trail. Maybe deer go this way. Maybe if you're lucky, you'll even see one. You find your heart beating a little faster from the excitement. You find yourself noticing how fresh and sweet the air smells. There is a bush ahead, flowering so profusely. Each pink blossom is exquisite, with its long stamens gracefully curving upward. Over the next rise, you see a flower whose long oval-shaped leaves show off its amazingly huge orchid blossom, shaped like the moccasin for which it is named. These beautiful flowers, which you never saw before, were so close to the old path. They have become visible only by taking the risk to go off the usual trail. You are aware of a new level of exhilaration within you, a renewed excitement about life. Now, there is a new trail with new possibilities.

You may find yourself experimenting with a number of new trails. Some will prove to be better than others, some more comfortable, some more exciting. Gradually, you may find yourself settling on one or two or three of the new ones, depending on what feels right in the moment. As you travel down them, they too may become more familiar and more well-worn. You may find yourself having to put less and less of a conscious effort into deciding not to go down the original path. That path is always available should you ever find a need to use it.

This is a metaphor of what actually goes on in our brains. Old habits have well-worn nerve-cell trails that go through our brain. These cell trails make it very easy to repeat old patterns of behavior. It is when we decide to change or add to our repertoire of actions that we need to stop and make a conscious choice to do something differently in order to carve out new cell trails.

The stories of L.W. and Christine powerfully remind us than it is more than okay to ask for help. Often, another point of view illuminates our own more completely and encourages us to expand our vision. When faced with the daunting task of changing, or a healing crisis occurs in our lives, we can benefit by responding fully and completely to the best of our abilities and to incorporate the excellent help that is found in dedicated healers, who offer a variety of interesting perspectives.

Another place to think about change is when you sit down to eat a meal. Are you are in such a hurry that you gobble down your food, hardly noticing what you have just eaten? Have you made a prayer of thanks for the energy exchange that the food on your plate offers your body, the life that has been given to support life? Have you taken the time to chew, to taste, and to take pleasure in this gift given to you and to the nourishment your body is receiving? Say you decide that you want to change this old habit. The first step has already been taken. You have noticed what you have always done unconsciously. You are paying attention in a new way and have brought a new level of conscious awareness to how you gobble your food.

You may want to pay attention closely to see how it happens. You may find yourself being distracted by such things as television, a tight schedule, worries carried from the day, or loud conversations. How can you change the steps of the old dance?

Maybe you want to sit down at the table more slowly, more consciously, shifting your attention to the food on your plate. Maybe you want to change where you eat, or maybe you want to eat together with your family. You begin to experiment with some new steps. You might try cupping your hands around your plate of food, or folding your hands in front of your heart, while giving silent thanks for the day and the nourishment provided before you. You may want to teach your children a new way, so you all hold hands around the dining-room table and each one takes a turn saying thanks for something that happened during the day, for the meal prepared, or the food which came from the garden. Maybe you make up a song to sing. There can be a number of creative and fun ways to experiment. After a while, you may find yourself gravitating to one or two of the new ways you have tried because they feel most right. At first, this took a lot of energy and focus: to stop, to notice, and to invent some new ways. After a while, as you settle down in the new routine and it takes less and less conscious thought. The newness has worn off, and a new habit has been formed.

The cycle of change takes place as you paused to notice some old way of being that was no longer satisfactory. You took the time to focus on your experience in order to discover exactly what the old habit was made of. Then, you began experimenting with some new ways. Creating some different responses felt awkward and unfamiliar at first, but gradually, you found yourself settling into one or two that worked the best. You expanded your repertoire and increased your ability to respond in more ways than the old tried and true. The old habits felt incomplete. As these new ways of behaving began to feel so much better, you became more confident in your ability to affect change in your life. These feelings became your reward for change and growth, and they served as your reinforcement for continuing to do them.

There was a time when I used ritual to help me release old patterns of behavior and discover some new ways of being. The conceptual framework from which I had viewed myself was shifting, and a new framework was beginning to form. I had set out to recreate the vision of who I was. I wanted to live out my heart's desire during the second half of my life.

I made a plaster mask of my face, like the mask I had worn for so long. It was the old face of yesterday, behind which I had unknowingly hidden for years. By paying attention, I had begun to see the old ways in which I was hiding. On the full moon after winter solstice, I built a fire and burned desert sage. I asked each of the four directions to join me and bring their sweet teaching gifts. Holding up the mask to each of the directions, I confessed out loud about how I had hidden for years. This confession helped me to come to a deeper understanding. Pitifully, I pleaded for help in releasing these old worn-out ways and asked for the courage to stand naked and unmasked before all.

I carefully laid the mask on top of the fire and danced around it in the growing heat. I asked the fire to release me at long last. The mask burned reluctantly. The fire pierced out of eye and nose holes. Slowly, the old disappeared.

A few weeks later, I visited my youngest son Marin in San Francisco. On the first day of the Aquarian Age, we went to Point Reyes, a beautiful National Park that overlooks the vast Pacific Ocean. We prayed with the sacred pipe: "May peace, love, and beauty be felt in the hearts of all of creation. May we be moved to take loving action in partnership with all aspects of creation to recreate balance and harmony here on earth."

As these prayers unfolded, I no longer saw myself as a child of God or as a servant of God. I saw myself as a co-creative partner with God. As an active participant, I had choices. I needed to listen carefully to my belly to see what felt right. I was an active, conscious, intentional, loving co-creative partner with the Great Mystery in the fullness of the present moment. A new age had begun, and the perceptions with which I had carried myself were to changing, too.

When I spent the night in the Sweat Lodge, on my birthday a few weeks later, I set that intention in motion. "I am a hollow bone, a conduit for the loving energy between God the Father and God the Mother. Like a lightning rod, I ground the light into the earth. I am a rainbow warrior of the light and of the heart, a seeker and seer of the truth. I am a healer, who helps to recreate balance and harmony where it has been lost."

In the lodge, the spirit of the snake reminded me to pay attention to my body, for every cell in my body already knew my purpose. I was to pay attention to the vibrations around me as well as those that move through me. I was instructed to be still, for I would receive all of the information that is needed. I saw myself standing in a shaft of golden light. My light body, much larger than myself, surrounded me. I knew that I was choosing to participate in the fullness of life and play my part in the cosmic dance that ushered in the new age of light.

I felt as if I had added to my knapsack of tools for my journey. My repertoire of ways of being in the world was expanding. Many of the old tools had taught me about how to be prepared and in control, and some had kept me well protected. After these weeks of prayer and ceremony, I knew that I had available to me all that I needed to be free and spontaneous in the present moment. I grew much more confident in my ability to affect the changes I needed in my life. My job was to pay attention and to trust my intuition. With open eyes, I saw and felt what was in me and around me. I was free to love and be loved.

> The dark tunnel pulls me down now,
> The luminous cave pulls me down now,
> Bear is there.
> Snake is there.
> Seven Grandmothers sit.
> Nights are long and beautiful.

5. Trusting Yourself

> A river runs through me
> bubbling and laughing,
> smoothing rough edges,
> cleansing
> every nook and cranny of my being.
>
> As this river pulls at my body,
> grown strong from countering the current,
> I lie back
> face to the stars,
> surrendering,
> trusting myself,
> trusting the river.
>
> The river runs through me,
> lovingly
> connecting me with *all there is.*

What if you truly trusted the abundant universe to provide for you every day, as you, in turn, gave back gratitude to the universe through all of your thoughts, actions, and feelings during the course of the day? To trust in the love and presence of the Divine in all things is to learn to trust yourself.

Trust is about words and actions matching over time. Trust or mistrust comes out of experience and is mended or destroyed through experience. You can no longer trust blindly through faith, belief, or obedience. You are being asked to learn to trust through your own experience.

A good place to start to learn about trust in the Divine is within you. Can you trust yourself? When you say you are going to do something, do you follow through? When you create an action, do you take responsibility for it in the words you speak? Do you stop to pay attention to what you are feeling and experiencing? How is the Divine Spirit moving in you at this very moment?

Take the time to notice your actions and your words. Look at yourself with fresh eyes. Sometimes it is helpful to go away to an unfamiliar place on a personal retreat. By taking time away from your usual routine and going to a place that is wholesome, you may gain a quiet time for yourself to read inspirational books, to write in your journal, take a yoga class or two, or meet, talk, and share ideas with other folks. You might come away seeing yourself differently and expand the dream of who you are.

6. Creating Positive Change

To heal is to change our way of being in the world through a process that brings us closer to a place where we are in a natural state of dynamic balance and harmony within. As we interact consciously with the world around us, we are able to flow with and respond to the present moment. Ultimately, we come to experience our divinity and oneness with all of life as we move the seat of consciousness from our minds to our hearts.

1. Heighten your awareness of your behavior and discover the ways that you act and feel, or your attitudes and perceptions that you carry that are no longer useful to you. Don't ignore the problems.
2. Without judgment and criticism, love all of you and patiently work to examine more fully those parts of yourself with which you are dissatisfied. Come to understand how those old patterns of response have served you.
3. Take the courage needed to begin to expand your repertoire of being. Experiment and explore some new behaviors, attitudes, beliefs, and perceptions, until you find what works best. Don't be afraid to ask for help. Actively participate in your search and discover the resources available to you. Be aware of your experiences and the results of your discoveries.

4. Learn to trust yourself by paying attention to your words and actions. Do they match over time? Personal integrity powers and enhances your self-esteem and sense of feeling whole and healthy in your body, mind, and spirit.

5. Love yourself with all of your strengths and all of your weaknesses. Learn to feel *divine love* emanating from your heart.

PART II

Creating the Prayer

CHAPTER V

Prayer

Be still and know that I am with you,
says the Lord.
Be still and know that I am you,
says the Tao.

We are a part of nature and nature is a part of us.
We are held by the Hand of God
and we are the Hands of God.

Do not try to live as if you are separate.
You are not.
You are of God,
part of the Tao.
You are within the landscape.
You are elements of the seasons.
Your are of both heaven and earth.

Be known for what you are, and make your actions harbingers of a
        better future.
Flow like the water round obstacles.
Do not batter your head against a brick wall.
Flow under it and when it collapses,
you will be gone.

Hold true to God
rest in the Tao,
and you will be carried to where the future needs you.

Martin Palmer[25]

---

[25] Elizabeth Roberts and Elias Amidon, eds., *Prayers for a Thousand Years: Blessings and Expressions of Hope for the New Millennium* (New York: HarperSanFrancisco, 1999), p.80.

1. The Structure of Prayer

One way to think about the basic format of the word "prayer" is to hold it as something very simple. First, you want to focus on the abundance in your life and express gratitude for all the beauty that surrounds you and that you feel inside. There may be people you would like to thank. I often acknowledge my teachers in prayer or a client who helped me see something new. You might want to thank the sun, earth, and rain for the food on your table. You might want to thank nature for the beauty around you.

When we had a short spurt of wonderfully warm rain in the early morning, I danced and sang in the rain a prayer of thanks to the cloud nations for providing water so life could continue. Another time, I was out working in my garden after the first real thunderstorm we had had in over a year. I was planting crops for fall and digging happily in the moist soil. I began a prayer of gratitude for the beautiful soil, the rain, the earthworms, and the seeds. After another thunderstorm two days later, I was out singing an impromptu prayer to the plants growing in my garden and to the nature spirits that care for those plants. I often express prayerful gratitude for the privilege of living among the trees and for guidance I receive. There are so many things to be grateful for.

Second, if you want to ask for help or a healing for yourself or others or even for the earth, it is helpful to be specific in your request. That way, there can be a specific answer. "Please, I need help to consistently have patience with my young puppy." "My stomach is in knots and my shoulders are very tense. I am feeling very stressed. Help me learn how to let go of the tension and anxiety I am feeling." "I am not feeling well. I have a headache and feel feverish. I am having difficulty focusing my attention. Please help me feel well again." "My friend is in the hospital. She is feeling very betrayed by a dear friend. Please bring her the help she needs to heal her heart." "Take this love I am feeling deep within my heart to the spaces and places it is needed on this earth."

Prayers can have a certain theme, like forgiveness or gratitude for a healing received or a meal about to be eaten. If you get some direction or guidance from prayers, which you have spoken, then it is a good idea to say, "Thank you," and to seriously consider this guidance, especially if it really resonates within you and feels right. Also, prayers may be spontaneous. At a certain moment, something moves you to say or do something. Prayers can take the form of an action, a song, or a dance. Consider that every action, every word, every thought, every move you make is part of a prayer you offer to the universe every moment of your life. The intention here is to raise your awareness to such a degree that all of who you are will go to the highest good of all of life everywhere.

You may feel much more comfortable praying for others. Praying for yourself may feel self-centered and egotistical. I encourage you to consider that you are as important as anyone else in your life. The opposite is also true. If you find yourself praying for just yourself, perhaps you need to consider others in your prayers. All of life, from the tiniest microorganisms to the largest blue whales in the sea, is interdependent. We can take nothing for granted. By acknowledging this connection, our interrelatedness becomes more apparent.

I have a client, who in his deepest desire to repair his marriage, has come to pray unceasingly: for his wife, for his step-daughters, for his marriage, and for himself. Overtime, he has learned to widen his vision of prayer and bring it into unselfish action. He goes to prayer groups at his church; he takes his turn caring for the little chapel; and now he has begun to volunteer up in the city with the nuns of Mother Theresa. The idea of going up to the city and possibly being in a bad neighborhood terrified him. Now, he cherishes every moment that he can sit in mass with them or help them care for the homeless or the shut-ins. He feels filled with peace and calmness, which he has never experienced before. He has let his prayers grow from focusing on himself and his personal situation to include many others who benefit from his giving, which, in turn, benefits him.

Praying for world peace is a good thing to do, but if you turn around and kick the dog or yell at your spouse or child or employee or yourself in the next moment, something is out of balance in your world. "World peace begins at home," says my favorite bumper sticker. Home can mean many things: your country, your family, your house and land, your heart. It is also important to think about the earth community. To "visualize peace" (another bumper sticker) is very powerful. What if everyone focused on creating world peace at home in their own hearts? Then, our worldwide goal might just be accomplished.

Visualization is an excellent tool for prayer and for creating your heart's desire. If there is a way of being in the world, which you want for yourself, take time to play with daydreaming about it. Become quiet and focused, breathing deeply and easily. See yourself as already having what you desire. Make a movie in your mind's eye, hear words or sounds or get a good sense of the energy that accompanies your desire. You can practice having fun by creating your dream. Let it emerge from a joyful place in your heart.

We had been experiencing quite a drought. In response, I prayed with my sacred pipe. "Was there anything I could do to help?" I had found myself worrying about the wilting dogwood and beech trees, not to mention the dying perennials in my flowerbeds. The answer seemed to come back, "Just love them." Later, I got the idea to love them by remembering them in the rain. So I began visually recalling my experiences with the trees, plants, and streams in the rain. Somehow, recalling these beautiful experiences felt much more helpful than being tied up in the energy of worry. It was a lot of fun, and not too many days later, the rains began to come.

The commercial development of a huge section of land in our county began with the tearing down of acres of trees. The smoke from their burning hovered in the sky as the bulldozers pushed and shoved the earth to change the contours of the land. In a Sweat Lodge ceremony, the suggestion was offered by the spirits to simply "imagine laying your hands on this scar in the earth and send out love to her." Just as I had done for the bad cut on my knee, "Imagine rubbing in the Vitamin E oil and gently nurturing the break in her skin back to health. The earth will prevail, especially with your loving support." Focusing on the beauty, strength, and endurance of the earth gave me a much greater appreciation for the cycles of life, death, and rebirth. I know that the sacredness of life will continue, and it feels very good to contribute my love to the process.

It is not appropriate to pray for someone else by telling God what you think that the person you are praying for ought to do. For example, this would not be the prayer to make: "Dear God, please let my son come to his senses and not buy a motorcycle." I don't have a right to presume to know what is right for my son. Now, I would discuss the issue with my son and express my point of view, but I have to recognize that, as an adult, he is in charge of his life. He needs to make the best decision for himself. I am out of my purview. I have no right to pray to try to make someone do something that I am sure is right. The same is true for a healing. You can pray for a healing for someone, for his or her highest good. You have no right to pray for how you think they should be healed or behave. You have no right to engage in doing a healing for anyone without his or her permission.

I might pray for my son in a slightly different way. I might say, "Dear God, please help my son find the transportation that is for his highest and safest good." Prayers for others are best when stated in the positive and in an open-ended fashion.

2. Creating Yourself as a Prayer

Take a few minutes to imagine what it would be like if you were living your life as a prayer. How would it feel? Really allow yourself to try it on for size. You might take the time to put on music that is very relaxing to you. Lie down in a comfortable place where you are safe, warm, and undisturbed. Close your eyes and tune into your body. Breathe deeply. Include as much of your whole body as you can into each breath. It is fun sometimes to imagine that the body is like a big balloon that you blow up slightly with each inhale and shrink back down with each exhale.

You can also start at your feet; be aware of them; compare the right with the left. Take the time to go body part by body part, moving sequentially up your body. Check everything out for temperature, tension, relaxation, color, feeling, and shape. Pay attention to the details and breathe into each part, letting go of excess tension, breathing in peace and relaxation and letting go of all that is unnecessary at this very moment.

If you find a spot where the tension is hanging on, it is helpful to hum into those muscles and bones. Actually, make a noise out loud and imagine the place where you want to release the tension. Do several deep breaths, hum and become aware of the sensation of vibration at that place in your body. As the tension subsides, move on to the next place and repeat the deep humming breaths. In this way, settle yourself down, so that there is a minimal amount of interference from your body.

Also, take the time to clear your mind. There are several ways to do this, all of which take practice. See your mind as a television screen or a radio. Watch your thoughts move across the screen, or listen to them as if the radio were on. Now, as if you had your hand on the brightness button or the volume controls, gradually turn up the brightness or the volume, until it is so bright or loud you can no longer see or hear your own mind. Now begin to turn it the other way, so the picture gets darker and darker or the volume gets softer and softer, so that, soon, there is neither picture nor sound. Maybe going out the brightness side works for you, or perhaps it's moving to the darkness to no picture. Experiment and see which does the best job of stilling your mind chatter.

You can also visualize putting all of your unwanted thoughts in a shoebox, tying it up tight and placing it in the back of a closet or in a safe-deposit box in your favorite bank. You can tell yourself that those thoughts are always available, whenever you need to have access to them. Now is just not the time.

Shift your focus on the present moment. What are you experiencing right now? Play music that is relaxing and comforting. According to research done at the University of California, at Irvine, Mozart[26] is particularly helpful because he chose to use certain harmonics that stimulate our brains in helpful ways. Climb inside whatever sound you choose. Be in the middle of it. Feel it reverberating through your body. Or get a drum, flute, or rattle and create your own sound. Let it help you settle into a larger sense of spaciousness and energy in and around you.

Another method to still the mind is to focus on a candle. Just watch the flame and the glow of the light getting bigger and bigger, again shifting your focus to the light connecting with you and filling you. Your job is now to bring a flashlight into the dark cave of your being and turn on the light of consciousness. When you choose to do this, you can no longer ignore what you see, feel, taste, touch, or think. You are asked to begin to take responsibility for your actions. Once you are willing to acknowledge the truth of what is happening, then you can make a conscious choice about what choices you might like to make.

Begin to move through the day in your mind's eye. Remember that you are imagining yourself living as a prayer. This might mean that you *see* yourself living with integrity; or it might mean that you *feel* what it is like to live in an open, honest, and loving way; or you may find yourself *hearing* words or sounds that support life as a consciously constructed prayer. There are different ways to

---

[26] Don Campbell, *The Mozart Affect* (New York: Avon Books, 1997).

experience things in your imagination. The key is to BE IN YOUR EXPERIENCE. Let go of all expectations. Be curious. Let it unfold before you. Don't try to control all of your experiences. This way, there will be room for more surprises. New things will creatively emerge.

Once you have tuned into your present self via your body, mind, and emotions, you can begin to set it aside and allow your imagination to play with the future. If you let your mind wander over the upcoming day, as if you were living your life already like a prayer, what would it be like? Let yourself play with that idea and see what might emerge as possibilities for living it as a reality. Set aside judgments and perceived limitations. Be there as long as you can maintain a focus. You may find yourself not being aware of outside noises, or you may maintain some awareness of your surroundings. It doesn't really matter. Have fun with it!

Sometimes fears have to be faced. I remember when I first started to learn to do relaxation techniques, I was afraid that if I really let go, my body would come unglued molecule by molecule, until there would be nothing left of me. I know now that the experience of having no boundaries and no form is very loving and very ecstatic. Over thirty years ago, when I didn't have a clear sense of myself, the thought of having no physical form terrified me.

Heightening our awareness of who we are at any moment in time helps to bring us into a place of dynamic balance and harmony and into living our lives as prayers. It is necessary to bring awareness into our present moment, in order to willingly choose how we wish to live this moment. This may seem like an awesome task. With perseverance and discipline, it is quite possible. No one can do it for you, so be lovingly patient with yourself. Every little bit of you counts, no matter how subtle. Each little bit is a step in the right direction. Something is better than nothing in this case. Remember that all is unfolding as it should.

When you find yourself back in full conscious awareness of your surroundings, take the time to pay *full* attention to them: your body, the room and its colors, shapes, and sounds. These may appear different than before. Just simply pay attention and notice the differences. If you have a fear that you will not find your way back to your room and your body, set an alarm or timer (a gentle one), or ask yourself to come back when the music is over. Wiggle your toes; stretch your fingers, your arms, and your legs. Gently move your head. Feel the blood, the warmth, and let the awareness return to your body.

Because you are likely to quickly forget your experiences, take the time to write them down. Coming out of a visualization session is like waking up from a dream. The dream, which seems so vivid at the time, is difficult to recall later in the day. When you write your experience down, you will remember more than you thought you did, and you may find yourself writing about a new awareness. The writing can take on a life of its own. Something of importance emerges out of being present to the process of writing.

So write whatever comes. You may gain more insights or more ideas. When your pen no longer wants to write, put it down. Reread what you have written. Or set it aside to reread later. Take from this experience the nuggets of gold. Begin experimenting with bringing conscious awareness to moments of your day. Begin to make increasingly conscious choices of how you live each moment.

What gets in the way of your living this way? What would have to change in your life now? We've looked at some of the fears that might come up. What are others? "People will think I am crazy." "I always need to play out the worst-case scenario, so I'll be prepared." If you are living more presently in the moment, then you are more able to respond to whatever happens. No scenario that you play out in your mind will come into being exactly as you worked it out. If, on the other hand, you work to develop confidence in yourself, your body, mind, and spirit, if you come to know yourself really well, then what do you have to fear? All of your faculties, your intelligence, your internal resources, your intuitions, and your connection to the Divine will be available to you in the present moment to help you meet the needs of the moment. What more could you ask for?

3. A Verbal Prayer

A personal prayer might go like this: "Ho, Great Mystery, you the creator of all things, this is your daughter, Claybasket. I come here this day with an intense feeling of gratitude for my life. You provide so much abundance. There is beauty everywhere I look. I am grateful for the gifts you have given me to share and the lessons you have brought my way. Even though these lessons are hard sometimes, you never give me more than I can handle. Thank you for the conversation with my friend the other night, as I struggle to create an internal framework for the celibate life that I am presently leading. Even though it is not what I had anticipated, I am grateful for the challenges of living by myself. Thank you for the strength of my physical body, which allows me to do the work that I need to do. Thank you for my work that sustains me not only financially but spiritually. Help me to always remember that I am never alone, that there are many seen and unseen helpers who accompany me. Help me to always take the time to stop and feel your love, which fills me without end. Help me to live fully in the present and not get caught up longing for a future that never is.

"I ask you to see my family; may the highest good come to them. May they be surrounded by the love that flows freely from my heart. Send my love to my mother, Cynthia, who has passed over. Thank you so much for all the people you send to me for healing. Thank you for their beauty and the lessons they so generously give to me. Help me always to be present to them in a healing way. Thank you for this beautiful place that you give me to live in, and the joy that I share with the Grandmother Earth, the devas, and nature spirits. May we always work well together.

"I am a conscious, intentional, active, loving co-creative partner with you living the prayer that is my life ever unfolding in joy and beauty in the present moment.

"Ho, Mitakuye Oyasin!" (All my relations!)

At the end of a therapy group, one of the women made the following prayer: "Dear God, thank you for these women who have come together to support me and each other. Thank you for their patience in listening to me. Thank you for their courage. Thank you for helping us to survive very difficult times. Please help us heal from the severe trauma inflicted upon us. Help us to learn to say no when it is appropriate. Amen."

At the beginning of Women's Circle, I like to create a prayer that moves around the circle, giving everyone a chance to speak out loud or silently from the heart. The prayers might go like this: "Ho, you, the grandfathers in the four directions, sky beings, and Grandmother Earth, hear our prayers. Thank you for this place where we sit. Thank you for gathering these women together. Give us the courage to be present for one another." "Thank you for my life. Help me learn to love myself." "Thank you for this circle of women. Thank you for this opportunity to pray, sing, drum, and talk." "I am feeling very lonely. Help me feel connected here." "Thank you for the bird songs. My life has been very hard this last month. Help me get the support I need." With each prayer, a little corn meal is offered to the fire as a way to give back some of what has been given to us.

These prayers are free flowing, responding to the impulse of the moment. They are created from the heart in the present moment and are spoken in the positive.

Prayers can also have a preset intention. The intention provides a template or framework. Heartfelt words are spontaneously spoken that fit within that framework. The Sweat Lodge ceremony is a good example. Feelings, thoughts, and desires are expressed in a specific order. As an apprentice to Sings Alone and Buffalo Woman, I spent years participating in Lakota Sioux Sweat Lodge ceremonies.

In the first round, you will hear the prayers addressing the different aspects of creation that come together to make this ceremony possible. Each of the four directions teaches us to pay attention in a particular manner. The prayers form around these teachings.

"You, Wakan Tanka, who are the creator of all things; you, the Great Mystery, we come to you in gratitude and humbleness. We wish to thank you for all that makes this ceremony, this day, this moment alive and beautiful and possible. Thank you for the spirits that guide us and fill our hearts and ears with words, feelings, images that help us to know the way. We acknowledge that the way can often be dangerous, mostly by our own making, as we let our egos get in the way of our true selves. Help us discern the truth. Thank you for the medicine helpers you send to us. Thank you for the many times their presence says, 'Pay attention. There is something important here.' Help us to take the time to listen. May we be a giveaway back to the people through the manner in which we live our lives.

"Thank you for each of the elements that go into making this ceremony possible. Thank you, Grandmother Earth, for opening your belly and allowing us to enter your womb. You hold us deep inside, keeping us safe, receiving us as we shed the old ways, old forms, and old patterns of behavior. You hold us while we prepare to be born anew, emerging out into the world once again. Thank you for lightning beings. You bring sharp, penetrating fire from the sky above directly to the earth below. Your masculine energy brings balance into this lodge. Thank you, Tree Nations. You give up your lives to hold the power of the lightning beings close to the stone people heating them red hot. These stone people get a little older and grayer each time. We welcome you one at a time into the womb of the Mother. You bring balance and wholeness here where we sit. We are grateful for your giveaway.

"Thank you, sacred herbs. Sage, you help clear the way by pushing aside the negative energy we have collected. Sweetgrass and cedar, you invite in the positive forces to surround us, protect us, and move through us. Tobacco, you help us have something to offer when we make our prayers. Corn, you are the life of the people. Thank you for these things, these aspects of creation that are like brothers and sisters to us. Help us to always acknowledge the help we receive and take nothing for granted. Help us to use these gifts in the manner intended.

"Thank you, water, for your breath of life. You are a gift from the cloud nations, collected in the rivers, lakes, and oceans as the lifeblood of the Mother herself. Without you, no life would be sustained here on earth. We bring your gift into the lodge, so that we can purify ourselves and receive you with much gratitude.

"Thank you to each of the four directions, sky, and earth. You to the west, you lead us deep down inside of our own being to the place of stillness where we connect with the Great Spirit. You bring the spirits to guide us. Help us this day. Lend your power here. Help us enter the silence, seek our own inner wisdom, and hear the voices of those who come to help.

"You to the north, thank you for the way you teach us to purify ourselves. You lead us to the ice lake when we seek the truth. You help us to see what we need to focus on in order to recreate balance and harmony in our own lives. Lend us your power here. Share your wisdom, so that we may walk in a good way.

"You to the east, thank you for the chance to begin again. Each new day brings us the truth and gives us the opportunity to bring awareness to our actions. Lend us your power here. Help us to walk the good red road with integrity and love. Shine your light into our faces and help us rejoice in the beauty that surrounds us and moves through us.

"You to the south, thank you for the dance with all my brothers and sisters around the sacred tree at the center of the Hoop of the Nations. Thank you for the reminder that we are all connected. Lend us your power here. Help us to remember that we are never alone. Help us to be aware of how every word we utter and every action we take affects our relatives (every aspect of creation).

"Sky beings high above—sun, moon, stars—thank you for the way you look down upon us, bringing us your guiding and loving presence. Lend us your powers here. Help us to walk our path of light by embracing our destinies with love, patience, and courage.

"Grandmother Earth, blessings to you. Thank you for welcoming us into your moist body. You open your very being to us so that we may learn to live and love and give away ourselves again. Thank you for your living example. Lend us your power. Help us to be available for whatever is needed whenever it is needed. Help us to learn to develop a respectful, honoring, caring, loving relationship with ourselves and with you. We enter into your body so that we can be reborn into a way of being that supports all of life. Have pity on us! We are simple two-leggeds, who need all the help we can get.

"We give thanks to our ancestors, who kept this ceremony alive, even at pain of death. They knew chaos would return, that we would need to pray in this manner. Thank you for my teachers, Sings Alone and Buffalo Woman. Help us to learn this ceremony well and pass it on to the next seven generations.

"Ho, Wakan Tanka, you the Great Mystery, connecting us all, we are grateful for your power and beauty. We are grateful for this ceremony of purification, which helps to bring us back into balance and harmony with ourselves and the universe.

"Ho, Mitakuye Oyasin!" (All my relations!)

As you pray from your heart, it is helpful to do so out loud so that all who are listening can give support. In this manner, healing can begin. These prayers can follow the images, thoughts, or feelings that flow from your conscious awareness.

"Ho! Wakan Tanka, the one that is a part of every living thing, I am grateful for my connectedness to *all there is* through you. I honor this day the tiniest microorganisms who are as essential to the sustainability of all of life as are the largest of the blue whales. Thank you for all of our brothers and sisters large and small, wild and tame.

"Please help me to understand my place in your divine plan. There are times when I act so pitifully, as if I was in charge of the whole universe. Help me to become aware of how I use every aspect of creation. Please help me to become fully aware of and support the interconnectedness and interdependence of all living things. Help me to understand that each species has a contribution to make to the greater good of the whole. Help me to understand how we can contribute to the highest good of all concerned. I give thanks to the last seven generations who not only kept the ceremonies alive, but also left enough of creation so that my life might be sustained today. They prayed for me so that I might stand strong this day in a sacred manner. Help me to learn how to meet the present-day challenges of sustainability, so that I will leave this planet even more beautiful for the next seven generations to come.

"Ho, Mitakuye Oyasin!"

Sometimes prayers come in the form of a story. If you are coming into the Sweat Lodge for the first time, the "White Buffalo Calf Woman" story is traditionally told. This story describes how the pipe came to the people. The prayer might go like this:

"Ho! You who are the Great Mystery, we are very grateful for the many ways in which you teach us. Thank you for the sacred pipe that you gave to us to carry as a sacred trust. With it we carry all of creation and are inseparably connected to it.

"Long, long ago, on a day much like today, the sky was bright blue, dotted occasionally with lazy white clouds. It was a time of chaos. The people had forgotten how to pray and had forgotten how to give thanks to those who offered their bodies so that the life of the people could be sustained. As a consequence, the soup pots were empty, and the people were very hungry.

"On this particular day, two brothers woke up early, determined that they would be successful in hunting. Today, they would become heroes among the people. They could feel it in their hearts. They would finally be the ones to find game for the soup pot. They set off over the prairie with hopes high and with a certain jauntiness to their step. They traveled a very long way and saw nothing. The only thing that moved were the blades of yellow-green prairie grass, which blew gently in the breeze. There was no game of any sort visible.

"Long into the afternoon, when their stomachs were growling and their feet were beginning to drag a little, they decided to sit for a while on a small rise. This place would give them a good view of the wide expanses. They sat for a long time in silence. A dark cloud of defeat started to slowly settle over them.

"Then they saw it. Hardly noticeable at first, off in the distance was a speck of dust. They felt their hearts leap to their throats and their bodies stiffen to alert. As they watched intently, the speck grew, and they knew that their luck had turned.

"Imagine their surprise when they saw it was a woman; not a buffalo or an elk, but a beautiful woman with long black shining braids hanging down over porcupine quills intricately designed into her white elk-skin dress. Each step she took was soft and carried with it great reverence for the earth. It was as if she caressed the grandmother with her feet. The light around her shone brightly. She was a marvel to behold.

"One of the brothers was quick to react. He said, 'Ho! A beautiful woman traveling alone. I will have my way with her. What luck for me!'

"The other brother was quite taken aback. 'Brother,' he said, 'can't you see that she is Wakan, sacred and holy?'

"It was too late, for the first was advancing toward the woman. Chest puffed out, proud of his manhood. A mist enveloped the man and the woman for what seemed to be a long time. When it parted, there on the ground, in front of the serene woman, was a pile of bones and rotting flesh and with maggots crawling in and out. Just as the stench reached the second brother she motioned him to come forward. Needless to say, he was a little reluctant, but did as he was asked reverently.

"'Go to your people,' she requested, 'tell them that I have come to teach what they have long forgotten. Have them set up a large council tipi and call all the families in from the outlying areas. I will be there when you are ready.' The young man ran back to his people as fast as his feet would carry him.

"In four days, the people who had been summoned arrived. A very large council tipi had been erected. All sat with great expectations around the council fire, for the story had spread like a spring storm among the people. So they waited.

"She came as she had promised. She walked slowly around the circle, looking closely at everyone. Few could look her in the eye. They felt a deep sense of shame. She spoke to them for a long time about how to pray, how to give thanks, and how to honor the gifts that they were given. That included the game they hunted and the food they ate. She reminded them about the interconnectedness of all things. She spoke to them about how to stand in their own truth side by side with the creator.

"Carefully, she lifted a red bundle from a beautiful leather bag and unfolding it said, 'Behold, in my left hand is the bowl of the pipe. It is made of red catlinite, a stone that holds the blood of the people. The bowl is round, open, and empty. It is the receptacle waiting to receive your prayers. With each pinch of tobacco, speak your hopes, sorrows, gratitude, and joys. Pray for love and peace for all of the people. Give thanks for what you receive.

"'Behold, in my right hand is the stem of the pipe. It is a gift from the tree nations. It is wrapped in leather from which a feather is hung. These signify those relatives, who offer to help you on your road. The stem is straight, thin, and strong. When fire is put to the bowl, it is activated by your breath as you draw it deeply inward.

"'The bowl and stem are meaningless when kept separate from one another. When they are joined, right to left, masculine to feminine, stem to bowl, they bring all of creation together as one. As the breath activates the fire, your prayers are released in the smoke, which rises upward. Wanbli Gleshka, the Golden Eagle, carries your prayers to the ears of the Creator.

"'It is important to walk your talk. Be thankful for the giveaway that makes your life possible. Be grateful for the abundance that is available to you as a gift from the Creator. What you do is not for yourself alone but is reflected in all of creation. If you choose to pick up a pipe made in the likeness of this one, know that you choose to live for the good of the people.'

"She took the time to teach them ceremonies in which the pipe is used. These were to help the people bring their lives back into balance and harmony. When she was finished, the people were filled with hope once more. As she left the tipi, the people, who were curious, followed her. But when a mist surrounded her, they stepped back, remembering what had happened before. This time, however, when the mist cleared, there was a young white buffalo calf rolling around in the dust scratching her back. Henceforth, she has always been known to the people as White Buffalo Calf Woman. As the calf ran off, they followed to see that the great herds of buffalo, elk, and deer had returned.

"For many generations, the soup pots have been full. Slowly, the people have once again forgotten how to live their lives in a prayerful manner. Chaos has returned and the world is out of balance. We are worried about the quality of our water, air, and food. We take endlessly from the earth and give back very little if at all. Help us to remember the teachings of White Buffalo Calf Woman so that harmony and beauty may return to ourselves and our mother, the Earth.

"Ho, Mitakuye Oyasin!"

In some traditions, prayers are completely formulated ahead of time. For example, prayers spoken during a church service are often written out ahead of time and come from a variety of sources like the Bible or philosophical commentaries. A number of my clients get a great deal of comfort and guidance from reading written prayers and guiding thoughts for the day.

I remember the time when I was driving across the country with my youngest son, who was about to begin first grade. I had been living in Vermont and had been accepted into graduate school in San Diego. Because nothing poisonous grew or lived in Vermont, the environment felt very safe. I was very familiar with the plants and trees that grew in New England. Now we were headed out into the unknown. I felt as if I might die, because in Southern California, the terrain was totally unfamiliar. Scorpions, sidewinders, rattlesnakes, black widows, and brown recluse spiders were abundant.

I had packed all of our belongings into my father's old steamer trunk and put it on top of my little green Pinto. I had carefully plotted a route across the United States that would avoid as much of the desert as possible. I had never been in the desert and the thought of it terrified me. On that trip, I found myself repeating the Twenty-third Psalm over and over. It came from childhood Sunday school memories, long before I was given the opportunity to study the Native American Red Road. It brought me great comfort and courage.

My little car crossed the Great Plains where we saw buffalo for the first time, crept slowly up the steep Rocky Mountains outside of Denver, and made it through the hot, arid land outside of Barstow, California. Barstow was not at all what I expected. My husband had described driving into California years earlier through lush green valleys. I was expecting green and got heat and miles and miles of barren sandstone. As near as I could figure it, he must have driven into

the San Fernando Valley, not the deserts of Nevada into Southern California. I
needed the comfort of the words in the prayer. I couldn't remember it exactly,
so I kept making up different versions. Whatever the form, it served me well.

Later that year, in the springtime, we went camping at Joshua Tree National
Park with a classmate of mine and his wife. He was a Marine who had done
desert-survival training. There were opportunities to learn about how the Native
American people of that area followed the acorn harvest, and how they used
certain plants to live on. Hiking among the beautiful exfoliated rock formations,
I discovered exquisite microenvironments that included flowering Beavertail
and Barrel cactuses. I saw rattlesnakes and learned how to treat snake bites.
Gradually, the desert became not only familiar but friendly and inviting. The
presence of the Creator was everywhere! More recently, I had the opportunity
to work with John of God, a famous Brazilian medium, when he came to this
country. When the space was being prepared for the day's healing, we were
asked to say the Lord's Prayer and the Hail Mary and then hold the "current,"
the very palpable energy field. The use of these two prayers stimulated me to
create one prayer that held the balance of the Mother/Father God.

> Heaven on Earth
> Our Father who art in Heaven,
> Our Mother who art in Earth
> Holy are your names.
>
> In sacred matrimony
> Do you come this day,
> Purifying our Hearts
> With love
> In thy holy communion.
>
> Blessed be to the Light of the One.
> May thy will be done on Earth
> As it is in Heaven.
>
> May thy love be
> Realized in the hearts
> Of humankind,
> And in all of life everywhere.
>
> For thine is the kingdom
> And the power
> And the glory,
> Now and forever more.
> So be it.

After I rewrote the Lord's Prayer, my friend Phebe told me that a direct translation from the original Aramaic language that it was created in went like this:

> O Birther!
> Father-Mother of the cosmos—
> You create all that moves in Light!

I find that very beautiful and very different from the current English translation that begins with "Our Father who art in Heaven." It is interesting how time and politics shapes reality.

4. The Body as a Prayer

Our bodies have been referred to as cellular cloaks and temples for our souls. They are the instruments, which, like a hide on a drum, give resonance to the beat of our lives. What choices do we make about how we care for these instruments? Based on the way we live, what are the notes we send to those around us? What kind of food, drugs, and/or alcohol do we feed our bodies? What kind of inner dialogue do we carry on about our bodies? When we look in the mirror, do we only allow ourselves to look at particular parts of our bodies in particular ways, or do we make derogatory comments to ourselves?

I used to suck in my stomach and run my hand across my belly to be sure that it was flat, grumbling if it was rounder than usual. It is hard in our present culture that demands such thinness to feel acceptable to really accept and love our bodies, and yet it is essential. We cannot profess to be loving persons and at the same time beat ourselves up on the inside about our thighs, faces, or hair.

As Americans, we tend to be obsessed with having the perfect body. For both men and women, there are very prescribed models, which we are supposed to look like. As a woman, do you really want to look anorexic like the fashion models? As a man, are the muscle-bound men in the magazines your ideal? What are the standards that you use to judge yourself against? How can you escape this prepackaging? How can you come to accept and love who you are in your present physical reality?

You can choose how you eat and exercise and how you care for your body. If you treated your body as a temple, how would you care for it differently? Your temple is structured differently from your neighbors. You are unique. Enjoy your uniqueness, your special form of beauty. The more you love yourself in a healthy way, the more radiant and beautiful you will become. Here are some ideas about how to shift your perceptions.

Pay attention. How do you talk to yourself? Notice first what you say and when you say it. Examine what you like about your inner dialogue and what you don't. Maybe you will discover that you use some pretty derogatory language. "You are so stupid." "How could you have done such a ridiculous thing?" "What made you think that you deserved something better?" "You look ridiculous in that dress." "That face is only something a mother could love." "So you're taking another bite. Aren't you fat enough already?"

When you find yourself talking badly to yourself, learn to stop and rephrase what you have just said in a more positive way. For example, "I want to learn how to do this better." "I need to take it more slowly." "I learn better by taking small steps." or "I am learning to like myself." "I really appreciate the healthy meal I prepared for myself tonight for dinner." "I am being mindful of every bite. It feels so good to take time to taste my food." "I am beautiful just the way I am."

You can offer a prayer to your body with every bite of food you eat. "Thank you for this food that strengthens and nourishes me." Food is nourishment to the body, mind, and spirit. It supports all of these parts of us. Plants, fish, and animals give their lives to support our bodies with the nutrients we need to be healthy and strong. It is an energy exchange. Take time to honor their gift to you.

As a result of modern farming and food-storage practices, much of the food that we buy at the grocery store lacks health-giving nutrients and vitality. We have to rely more and more on supplements to supply us with the vitamins and minerals we need. I highly recommend that you buy organic produce whenever you can. Better yet, turn your lawn into an organic vegetable patch. You would be surprised how much you can grow all year round, and how good it tastes when it comes fresh from the garden to your table. When I lived in New York City, I had a garden on the roof. In Vermont, I pulled carrots, rutabagas, beets, and parsnips fresh from the ground all winter. In Maryland, I can keep kale and Chinese greens growing all winter long. It is a very satisfying endeavor and good therapy for the soul to work in harmony with the earth and to invite the nature spirits back to the land.

Eating food allows us the pleasure of nourishing our bodies and our energy. It is an energy exchange between the plant and animal nations and us. It is their gift to us. Some take great joy not only in how the food tastes, but also how it is presented on the plate and the quality of the nourishment offered. It becomes a work of art and a joy for the cook and the consumer.

If you have to follow your meals with Tagamint or some other antacid, then you might consider changing your consumption to foods that are more congruent with your body. The plants in the garden are not eaten by bugs or are not susceptible to so many diseases if the soil is well balanced. The same is true with your body.

It is important to take the time to look not only at what you eat, but how you eat. Do you take the time to say thanks? Do you eat slowly enough, so that you can appreciate the myriad of flavors? Do you chew well, so your digestive system can begin to mix saliva and digestive enzymes, breaking down the food in your mouth?

Are you watching television, or are you sitting with your family, having a nurturing, supportive "what happened in your day" sort of conversation? People seem to think that zoning out in front of the television when they come home from a hard day is mindlessly restful. If this is truly what you need, pay attention to what you watch. So much of the programming is filled with negativity and violence, especially the news. Is this truly restful and replenishing? Constructing a bridge between work and home life can be very helpful. Maybe taking a walk with your family or by yourself or turning on some very soothing music, doing a few exercises after you have smudged with sage, or meditating or working in the garden touching the earth would give you more of what you are looking for.

Saying grace before a meal helps remind us how much we are a part of a greater whole that supports all of life. Tibetan doctors recommend a prayerful meditation before taking medicine, because it makes the medicine that much more powerful for the body. Perhaps the same is true with the food we eat. As we say grace, we can see this food as beautifully vital, blessed with *divine energy*. We might even envision the energy and light coming into our bodies as a sacred gift. We can say thank you to all that is for the people who gather around the table, for special events that occurred during the day, for a gift given or received, for the dance of the sun and earth that make the bounty that we put into our bodies, for the hands that made our food, for those that give away their bodies to feed ours. A Native American tradition is to prepare a spirit bowl into which you place a bite of everything that you are about to eat. This bowl is then placed out on the earth to thank the spirits, who so generously guide us. Thanks for their guidance are included in the prayer for the meal.

If our bodies are temples, how can we treat them in reverent manner? Do we hold our bodies in unnatural positions, like sitting at a desk for extended periods of time? The intricate design and function of the body is a miracle. To honor the body means to take good care of the delicate balance that keeps us healthy. Exercising is helpful as long as it is an exercise program that listens to and treats our organs, bones, and muscles kindly. There are many systems of exercise like yoga, aikido, and tai chi that honor our bodies that move slowly enough to allow feedback from our bodies. Feeling the feedback from bones and muscles lets us know when we've done enough or directs us to a part of the body that is asking for special attention.

The body was formed from dust or clay, according to some stories. It is mostly water and contains a molecular structure similar to our environment. In a certain sense, our bodies are of the earth. I see my body as the earth's body and the earth as my body. It is interesting to think of it this way. Do we treat our bodies and the body of the earth the same? Maybe it would be a good thing to bring some loving kindness into the formula, offering our bodies as prayers for beauty and wholeness, just as we love the earth and all of her beauty.

Our bodies can also be powerful teachers. Care of my body began long ago, when I made the decision in college to dance professionally. I stopped smoking and drinking alcohol excessively. I began to exercise regularly, by taking as many dance classes as I could. However, my energy was jagged, with uneven ups and downs, because I was relying on candy bars to give me energy and yogurt to keep me thin. Someone suggested that I try a whole-grain vegetarian diet. I was willing to learn and began to read books to find new ideas. When I put these ideas into practice, my energy patterns shifted dramatically. I was able to consistently sustain high levels of energy without the old ups and downs.

As soon as I finished college, I went straight to New York City. I had dreams of becoming a famous dancer and choreographer. One particular day, during one of the floor exercises in a class with Merce Cunningham, I badly injured a muscle in my back. A friend of my husband's happened to be in class that day. She told me that she knew some exercises that would help me, but I would have to stop dancing for a while. Learning to release the tension in my muscles would teach me how to move more freely. This decision was not easy. I was very involved in the avant-garde movement in modern dance at Judson Church in the Village and was a member of the James Waring Dance Company. My career, which was beginning to take off, required that I take several dance classes a day and attend rehearsals at night. But the truth of it was that I was injured and something had to change.

I decided to begin an apprenticeship with Elaine Summers, who taught me a system of rehabilitative exercises called Kinetic Awareness. The exercises were designed to relax muscles, open more spaces between bones, increase the range of motion, and ultimately create more freedom of movement. This is similar to the work of Moshe Feldenkrais.

My body became an incredible teacher for me, as I began to learn to pay attention and sustain long periods of very quiet focus. I isolated the movement of each muscle, so that if I chose to move my right arm in a certain way, my neck, head, shoulders, and ribs wouldn't follow old patterns of inclusion but would remain still. I brought my conscious awareness into every part of my body and developed a breathing and humming technique that helped me to relax and focus. Slowly, I was able to learn how to move without all of the old tensions. My body, as an instrument, was becoming more finely tuned.

I did not understand how much releasing the old patterns of movement in my body would affect my whole world. My dances changed from cleanly choreographed lines to the organic flow of kinetic images and improvisations that responded to the present moment in time, space, and rhythm. My husband, Malcolm Goldstein, who is a violinist and composer, and I performed often in a partnership of music and dance.

One night, I dreamt that I was Ruth St. Denis looking for a performance space. The place chosen was a small rectangular trellised platform that was like a temple in a meadow. Using the dream as an inspiration, I chose to make a dance that did not move out into the space. With my body as my temple, I quietly moved in whatever way my breathing and body called for in the moment. I wore a beautiful long 1930s dress given to me by a friend. It was cut on the bias, so that the silken fabric revealed the subtle movements. Another woman designed my headpiece. Long streamers, dotted with disks containing mirrors, hung from a band around my head. One time, I performed this piece in an old warehouse in the area that is now Soho. The warehouse was serving as a movie theater for experimental film. The house was dark. I took my place and began a toning meditation that helped me center. When the lights went up, there was a black cat sharing the stage with me. He joined the dance. When the light reflecting off the mirrors on my headpiece danced in space, so did he. When the lights went out, he disappeared. What a mystery.

The kinetic-awareness work that Elaine taught me became a major turning point in my life. The groundwork was laid for later emotional, psychological, and spiritual development. I had learned to slow down, to focus my attention, and to move from the inside out rather than be caught up in the external form. At the time, I had no idea about what was to come but simply continued to explore new ways to dance.

Paying attention to your body can lead to living a much healthier life. We have a harmful reflex in this culture. If it hurts, take a pill to make the pain go away. But what you make go away is your signal, the message, which your body is sending you. Pain indicates that something is wrong and in need of attention. When there is an infection in the body, a fever is created to help burn the infection away. A knot in your stomach may be telling you that you are very anxious about something and need to slow down to take care of whatever it is.

Our bodies are incredible miracles, delicately balanced, intricately put together, and wonderfully able to absorb and ameliorate so many of the stresses and strains that come from living. Take good care of yourself.

Honor yourself.

Feed yourself well.

Talk to yourself in a kindly manner.

Orient yourself toward preventative health care and wellness.

Get massages and go for good walks.

Let your body and the body of the earth come in contact with each other in a way that benefits both. Enjoy life through the sensory vehicle, which your soul has been given for this passage of life in three-dimensional reality. In short, treat yourself in a sacred manner. Your body is a valuable part of the prayer that you offer to the Great Mystery.

5. Meditation

Meditation has been described as a journey from the surface mind to the undifferentiated mind by progressively extending calmness and awareness to more and more subtle levels. The meditative experience leads to moments of insight, which brings with it a radical shift and permanent change in our perspective.[27] Eknath Easwaran, who translates spiritual ideals into daily life through meditation, says, "By changing the very mode of our thinking, we can remake ourselves completely."[28] By moving into inner silence, we learn to listen differently and touch the God-self within. Meditation is a wonderful tool to use in consciously constructing ourselves as living prayers.

There are a number of ways to meditate. Experimenting with a wide variety of techniques helps you to find those methods that work best for you. The method of meditation that fits your primary learning style (kinesthetic, visual, or auditory) will most likely work best for you. I am a kinesthetic learner, and when I was taught meditation techniques, I thought for a long time that I was not doing it right. I could not "see" pictures like my sister, Starfeather, who is very visual. She was getting Technicolor movies, while I would get vague hints of images and a lot of "sensing," "knowing," or feeling the information.

I also had a great deal of difficulty entering the silence. There were too many conversations going on in my head and too many distractions, like the ache in my back or an external sound in the room. And of course, I had a series of expectations about what meditation "should" be like, which were shaped by books I read on the subject. Some of these expectations involved how quickly I was supposed to progress toward Nirvana or oneness with God. I had put myself on the fast track that only served to slow things down even more. Over the years, I have learned to accept what is and not push the river. Meditation has become a great deal more enjoyable as a result.

There are some simple preparations that can help to minimize distractions while meditating. Eating lightly (no caffeine or sugar) or not at all, prior to your practice, keeps the body and mind calmer, more open, and receptive. When night changes into day or day into night are particularly powerful times to practice. But given most people's busy schedules, whenever you can manage to get twenty to thirty minutes of quiet time is a good time. Smudging, a Native American practice of surrounding the body with the smoke of desert sage, cedar, and/or sweet grass, helps to clear away the cares of the day and invite in positive energy. In Eastern practices or during Catholic mass, incense is used for the same purpose. Using incense or lighting a candle or ringing a chime helps us step out of our ordinary life into a special time that is set aside for connecting more deeply with the sacred.

Breathing techniques are keys to relaxing, shifting attention, and focusing. There is a powerful meditation practice, which is nothing more than paying

---

[27]   Elizabeth Roberts and Elias Amidon, eds., *Earth Prayers from Around the World* (New York: HarperSanFrancisco, 1991).

[28]   Eknath Easwaran, *Meditation* (California: Nilgiri Press, 1978, 1991, p.11).

detailed attention to our breathing. Normally, we tend to breathe very shallowly. By controlling the length and depth of each breath, we learn to control our minds. A meditation practice helps to disengage our minds from normal, everyday activities. Through this process of disengaging our minds, we shift our perspectives and allow the possibilities for new insights.

Shifting our perspectives can come by simply doing an everyday activity differently, like changing the way in which we breathe. In his book, *Mindfulness with Every Step*,[29] Thich Nhat Hanh encourages us to use washing the dishes as a meditation practice by paying detailed attention to the process. Simply by stepping outside of our ordinary reality by doing any common activity differently facilitates changes in our way of seeing and being.

Experience moving, making music, singing, walking, or drawing differently. For example, if you are right handed, draw or write with the left. Pay attention to what you are doing and, as a result, heighten your conscious awareness of what you are doing and how you are being. There are doorways hidden in a simple gesture or vortex of energy that open the gates to higher states of consciousness.

Draw with your left hand (if you are right handed), or cut out a circle and paint within this sacred symbol.

Put on slow repetitive music, like the music of Gabriel Roth,[30] and begin to let the music come inside your body and be moved in response to it. Pay attention to what is happening. You are an inside experiencer, who is not controlling the body and its movement, nor criticizing what you see or feel.

Go for a silent walk in the woods, move off the path, and sit for a long time in a secluded spot observing and feeling everything.

Make a drum or rattle, take it outside where no one can see you, make sounds and feel your feet on the earth. Start singing anything that comes to mind. Let new words, sounds, tones, or notes flow out of your mouth. Surprise yourself as you listen to yourself, without judgment.

Here are two very powerful meditations that bring balance and harmony to the body, mind, and spirit. They can help you create a flow between your heart and the universe. They are amazingly easy ways to fill yourself with the love of God and the divine essence that flows through us all. They can be done together or separately, alone, or with others.

A toning meditation: Feel your feet touch the earth and hum into her belly. Hum deep into the center of her being. Imagine that her heart is a beautiful turquoise color, green and blue living in the center. It pulsates her radiance ever outward and inward in a rhythmic drumbeat. Baboom . . . baboom . . . baboom . . . baboom!

---

29   Thich Nhat Hanh, *Mindfulness with Every Step*.
30   Music by Gabrielle Roth and the Mirrors: Waves, Luna, Trance, Refuge, and Bones.

Hum a low tone into her heart. Feel the vibration of that tone as it connects the two of you through your feet.

Shift your focus to the base of your spine and hum into this place that is called your root chakra. Feel the energy center as you hum into this part of yourself. You may see a red light pulsing from this place or feel a vibration in your body. Send your humming sound by attention to this place or pitch a low note that increases the sensation of vibration at the root of your spine.

After several deep humming breaths that have connected you well with the root chakra, then move your attention to your belly just below your navel. Pitch a slightly higher note or simply hum. Feel the vibration inside. See an orange color. Sometimes, I like to imagine that there is a rose the color of the chakra sitting in that space in my body. When you have connected well at the second chakra by feeling the vibration in that area of your body, move to the third, or solar plexus, just above the stomach under the diaphragm. Raise the pitch of your sound or continue the humming breathing. Feel the vibration shift to your solar plexus. You may also experience a yellow color. Then move to the fourth chakra at your heart and notice a green or pink color. You may want to include an increasingly important center at the thymus, just above the heart. The thymus is an integral part of your immune system. As you continue, create a higher tone or a simple hum, which sets up a vibration at the fifth chakra at your throat, and you may notice an indigo blue color. Coming up to the sixth chakra, your pineal gland, or third eye between your eyebrows, feel the vibration and you may notice a violet color. Reaching a high tone or hum, feel the spot on your crown where your soft spot used to be when you were a baby, feel the vibration and at your crown and visualize a white color. You may or may not experience the colors. Take the time to adjust your tone or place your hum in each energy center so that you feel vibration there. Your energy will follow your attention and your awareness will increase.

If you have more time to spend, you can include the energy centers outside of your body. There is one at the etheric body level, just a few inches up from the crown. Often, when you tone here, it feels as if it excites an electrical field running around your whole body close to the surface. The next is at the edge of your light body.[31] Imagine that you emanate a radiance of light so beautiful that it extends well beyond your physical body. Pitch a tone high into that light and feel its resonance around the luminous egg that is an extension of your physical form. Once you have connected, move to a higher pitch, which brings you to the sun. Imagine that you are the sun, powerful, radiant, nourishing the earth

---

[31] According to Richard Gerber, MD, in *Vibrational Medicine* (Santa Fe: Bear and Company, 1988, 1996), the light body is made up of subtle energy bodies that surrounds and interpenetrates the physical body. The subtle bodies are the etheric, astral, mental, causal, and higher spiritual aspects of the multidimensional human form which exist in higher frequency octaves.

with your energy, nourishing the whole solar system with your light. See the planets dance around you. Feel your movement in the larger dance of the Milky Way. Last of all, pitch a tone as high as you can imagine. It took me a while to open up to each of these higher tones. Be patient and practice them. This highest one includes the universe and beyond. It is about being the one verse that is all things. It is about the possibility of encompassing in conscious awareness a multidimensional reality.

Complete this meditation by toning down the scale from highest to lowest, or humming into each center, visualizing each place as you touch into it, and ending deep within the earth.

The energy centers in your body will be opened and energized. You will probably feel more centered and grounded. Take the time to notice your experience and describe it yourself.

The Balance Dance, a moving meditation: Begin in a quiet place, preferably outside on the earth. If you can't get there, your office, living room, or any other place will do. Be sure there is a little bit of space cleared around you, and know which way is north. Begin by facing north and moving to each of the four directions in a clockwise manner, going to the east next, then south, then west. You can do just one sequence in each of the four directions or four sequences or multiples of four. Maintain a focus on your movement, not on grocery lists for tomorrow. I will give you some imagery to work with. After a while, give up the words, too, and just be in the moment of creating the flow of movement and connection with the *divine energy*.

Pay a great deal of attention to your breathing and coordinate the breath with the movement. Your breathing enhances the flow of the movement and your ability to exchange energies with the earth, heavens, and the balance and harmony that fill you up. In turn, you give away this loving energy, only to be filled up again and again. Beauty and grace are contained in the flow of the receiving and giving, one generating the other in a continuous circular flow.

Standing with your feet parallel, let out your breath as you move to touch the earth (which may sometimes be represented by the floor) with your hands in front of you. As you touch her body, feel her heart, her strength, her beauty, her ability to nourish you so completely. Slowly breathing in, while rolling up your back and keeping your head loose, move your hands from her body, feeling your fingertips leaving the texture and temperature of her, as if there are strings still attached to her that are reeled out as you straighten up. These strings or lines of energy encompass your toes, your feet, your ankles, your calves, your knees, thighs, pelvis, abdomen, and ribcage as you bring your hands to your heart. Feel the energy from the Earth Mother filling your heart. Exhale and inhale slowly. Take the time to receive the gift of the Earth Mother into your heart.

Again put your attention into your fingers. Breathing out, slowly reach your fingers to the sky. Be aware of the power of the sky and sun and space. Imagine that you can touch them with your fingers. Feel the masculine power, directed, strong and warm. Inhaling, pull this power, this light, this energy down through the crown of your head, to the head, neck, chest, and fold your hands over your heart. Breathe the energy of the heavens into your heart and receiving it, let it fill you up. Let the breath flow out.

Breathing in, open your arms and feet to the side, with your toes pointing comfortably away from your body and knees slightly bent. Your right hand moves up and to the side, until it is just above the level of your head to the right of your body, with your palm and facing forward, and your fingers open and extending skyward. Your elbow is slightly bent. Your left hand moves out to the left side, just below shoulder level, elbow bent, palm forward, fingers extended toward the horizon. As you breathe out, feel the balancing between the right and left sides, between the masculine and feminine, between doing and being, between opposites of all kinds. Breathe in as you draw the love and peace that is generated from balancing these opposites, bringing your hands once again to your heart, receiving that peace and love into your heart, your being.

As you breathe out, extend your hands forward to make an offering. Give away your breath, your love, your sense of peace and harmony to a specific person, to a tree, plant, neighborhood, earth, the atmosphere, the universe, to whomever or wherever feels right to you. It is your turn to give away your unique gift of all the beautiful life-giving energies that you have gathered together. Give it all away freely, unconditionally. Then replenish yourself again by reaching down to touch the earth and repeat the sequence.

My sister, Starfeather, likes to do this in a circle of people gathered around a medicine wheel. She does the sequence seven times: once to the center, once to each of the four directions beginning with the north, once focusing energy to the earth and once to a specific person. When facing the center, focus on sending the energy to *all there is*. As you turn to a direction that places you facing the back of another person, send the energy to that person, at the same time, you are receiving it from the person behind you. When facing away from the circle, focus your energy on the community in which you live.

If you have time to do four times in each of the directions, focus on the teaching of that particular direction. During the first couple of times in a particular direction, you may hear words in your mind that form a prayer. The giveaway may be focused on a particular person, plant, tree, community, or any aspect of creation that you feel calls for your attention. It is important to note here that you do not name specifically how something needs to be healed. Your purpose is to send energy from the highest levels of love and peace and to let go of the outcome. We are learning to give love unconditionally, without strings attached.

Here is how each of the four directions might be used. Starting in the north, allow the cold winds of the north to purify your entire being. Begin to wash away that which holds you back from being the best you can be, giving it up to earth and sky, drawing their energies to clear you and to help you live in balance and harmony. It is out of this place of balancing right and left, masculine and feminine, dark and light, that wisdom flows freely out to wherever you choose to direct it.

Turning to the east, having shed the old unwanted disharmonious patterns, you are like a newborn, standing in the light. Draw in the light of the earth, the sun, moon, and stars. Bathing in this light, feel the growing strength of your own light. It is this truth of who you are becoming in this moment, the radiance of your own being, fed by earth and sky, that you freely give away from your heart in the east.

In the south, you discover that you are never alone. Your connection to all aspects of creation continually feeds and is fed by your life's dance here on earth. The smallest microorganisms to the largest blue whale, the tinniest spring flower to the towering ancient redwood, all aspects of life are interrelated and interdependent. In this place, you can use your connection to earth and sky, and your place of balance between them to feed the love of the heart to all of creation, much in the same way all of creation feeds you.

Facing the west, the focus is to empty yourself of all extraneous thoughts and feelings, to give them up to the earth and sky as you reach to each of these directions, drawing the power of silence into your body, touching into the divine essence that is you at the very core of your being. When you come to the place of balance, you are clear, openhearted, beautiful, ready, and willing to receive the guidance that comes from aligning yourself with your higher self, your soul's intention, and your spiritual ancestral heritage. Now you are ready to give all of it away, quietly, openly, and peacefully. You have brought in the strength, power, courage, and support from sky and earth, to give away a love that flows unconditionally from your heart.

Give away this love that you collect in your heart to a person, place, thing, or to the whole universe. The more you do this dance, the more you will discover that this love is like a clear mountain spring, ever flowing. And words will become less important as you move within the flow of the Divine.

6. Creating Prayers for Others

There are a few important cautions to use when creating healing prayers for others. For example, you may determine, in your infinite wisdom, what you think other people need. Maybe you know them well and think that if only they would do such and such, they would get better. Humbly, you, I, or anyone else does not have the power to change another person. Maybe, for example, someone is very ill. You pray for her to live, and instead, she dies. Perhaps this person's soul has called for something different than what you wished. Maybe dying is exactly the best thing that could happen to that person, but your emotional attachment calls for something different out of your own need. Although we do not have the power or prerogative to decide what is best for another person, we can pray for the highest good to come to this person, and we can send them a great deal of love.

Much to my dismay, my youngest son has wanted a motorcycle for a long time. He assured me that if I saw him ride his bicycle in the streets of San Francisco, I would be glad to have him on something more substantial. Somehow this wasn't reassuring, so I decided to say a prayer for him. It was clearly not my prerogative to pray that he not get a motorcycle. I really wanted him to get something safer. So I formulated my prayer as follows:

"Ho, You, who are the Great Mystery, hear my prayer. Thank you for the life of my son. He is beautiful and strong. He stands behind his words and is willing to take action for things that are deep in his heart. Thank you for the privilege of being his mother. He needs good, safe, inexpensive transportation. Please help him find what is in his highest good. Ho, Mitakque Oyasin!" He purchased a motorcycle. Maybe that was what was best for him, I don't really know. I accepted that, and my prayers shifted to his safety. "Creator of All Things, thank you for the beauty of my son. Help keep him safe in his travels." He took a motorcycle-safety course and was doing very well. When he could afford it, he sold his motorcycle and bought a truck. I was grateful and needed to let go of a process I had no control over.

When you make a prayer for someone, ask for the highest good to unfold for that person. This way, it is left in the hands of the Creator to determine what lessons this soul needs rather than you dictating what should happen. Sometimes, when I am praying for something for myself, I ask for that to happen or something better. Maybe my imagination is limiting more exciting possibilities.

To pray for peace and healing for a certain country or the earth is an opportunity to contribute your loving energy in that direction. As with all prayers, the idea is to get your ego out of the way and simply be a conduit of the loving energy from God the Father and God the Mother. You can direct that unconditional love to someone or something and know that you are participating in the most powerful healing possible.

I often imagine setting up a column of light in cooperation with the deva of the earth, the Overlighting Deva of this property, nature, my guides, my higher self, and medicine helpers (usually animal helpers). This is my *earth healing* team. I set the intention and imagine a golden column of light that reaches deep within the belly of the Mother and high up into the sky above. I open my heart, feeding this light the love I feel for the Divine, for the earth, for this land, for the trees, for my dog, who is always present, and for anything or anyone who comes to mind within that moment. I feel this light resonating, vibrating with beautiful loving energy. Sometimes, a particular place on the planet comes to mind, and I focus my attention there. Sometimes, I simply state, "I am available" and imagine that this light is functioning like an acupuncture needle, restoring balance and harmony wherever needed.

One afternoon, I met with four women friends. After a good lunch, a little pleasurable shopping and a delightful movie, none of us wanted to stop our fun, so we came to my house to dance. At one point, someone suggested that we put my dog, Athena, in the center of our circle. She was getting old and wobbly. We danced around her, pouring out our love for her. The next day, her coat was shiny, her eyes sparkly, and her gait uplifted. There had been no plans, no expectations, just the present moment, a spontaneous intention, and lots of love flowing all around. We returned to her the kind of unconditional love that she had freely given during her entire life.

Interesting studies with groups of patients, who were quite sick, demonstrate the power of prayer. Unbeknownst to the patients, one group was prayed for, and one group was not. The group that was prayed for showed marked improvements. Prayer is very powerful. Be careful not to slide into needing proof of your efforts. Pray without attachment to the outcome. The prayer is a holy feeling of love expressed by you to another. That love is beautiful in and of itself.

7. Prayer

Prayers can have many forms. Every action we take, thought or feeling we generate, and every word we speak are parts of the prayers we constantly offer to all of life. By heightening our awareness of our bodies and minds, we can powerfully and consciously construct ourselves as living prayers.

1. First, focus your prayers on the abundance and express your gratitude for all of the beauty that surrounds you and that you feel inside, and then ask for help or for healing for yourself, others, your community, or the earth community.
2. Visualization is an excellent tool for prayer and for creating your heart's desire.
3. Have fun imagining that you are living your life as a prayer. Spontaneously create personal prayers that help guide your growth and spiritual development.
4. Fine tune your body as a beautiful instrument of prayer by becoming more aware of your physical self and appreciating the beautiful miracle of your human body.
5. Use meditation to shift your perspective and gain insight.
6. Create prayers for others that help to direct your love unconditionally to them for their highest good by letting God handle the details of what that means.
7. Just let it all go and become the living prayer.

CHAPTER VI

Beginning Your Day

"The mountains, I
become part of it . . .
The herbs, the evergreen,
I become part of it.
The morning mists, the
clouds, the gathering
waters,
I become part of it.
The dew Drops, the
pollen, I become
part of it."

Navajo Beautyway Chant[32]

1. Opening Your Day in a Prayerful Manner

Are you in charge of your life, or is someone or something else in charge of you? Technology was originally created to help us so we would have more time to play and create. The opposite has happened for most people. We have responded by going faster, trying to do more and more, until we make ourselves sick in our bodies, minds, and spirits. Are you living life the way you want to? Does your lifestyle truly nourish you at your highest potential? Take the time to put yourself in charge of your day and create it in the best way you know how.

The way you begin your day is very important. It sets the tone for the rest of the day. Here are some suggestions.

Lie in bed quietly, honoring the transition from dreamtime to wake time. Think back over your dreams. Take the time to write down the important ones. Later on in the day, you can spend some time discovering what they mean.

---

[32] *Navajo: Walk in Beauty, Native American Wisdom* (San Francisco: Chronicle Books, 1994), p. 34.

Before you jump out of bed, think over the things you have to do that day. Begin to organize them. If you're feeling overwhelmed, make a list and prioritize them. Be sure to keep a good balance between doing and being. Set an intention for the day, and put it into prayer. One of my meditation students says he waits until he smiles, only then does he get out of bed.

For years, I put on Gregorian chants and did yoga. I'm not sure why this particular combination appealed to me, but it worked to slow me down and move me peacefully into the day. I was a very speedy person, and I needed to change the way I started my day.

Often, I will go out into the woods at first light, or even while it's still dark, to simply sit. This is such a holy time, as night turns to day. It is beautiful to watch the change of seasons in the life cycle of the trees, birds, and insects. I may, or may not, say a formal prayer. When the first rays of sunlight catch my eye, I sing an old Lakota song to greet this radiant being. Sometimes, I will do chanting or toning or drumming. It depends on what I am moved to do at the time.

Recently, I set up an altar in the garden in front of my house. It is here every morning that I offer cornmeal and thank the Great Spirit for life, for the standing ones, and for my four-legged companions. Especially, I thank the devas and nature spirits, who have created such beauty all around me and who have helped me in so many ways.

I have experimented with several other ways to start in the morning. They help me center myself and open the energy centers in my body. I put on a recorded tape of Vedic chants. I sing along with these chants, which are directed to each of the seven energy centers in the body. Or I might do the toning meditation I described earlier. Another simple and very powerful technique I use is deep-breathing exercises. By breathing in and out deeply for the same length of time or exhaling for twice as long as breathing in while lying on the floor or sitting with my spine straight, I create a deep sense of connectedness with all of life. This exercise can be done while driving to work. Our breathing patterns create our internal rhythm more than anything else. If you want to change what you are experiencing at any moment in time, change the way you are breathing.

Get enough sleep the night before so that you don't have to jolt yourself awake with sugar, coffee, or soda.

Flower essences are another tool for supporting your electrical system. These help coordinate body and soul. Take vitamins. Eat a nourishing breakfast. Thank the earth and sun for the chance to begin a new day and for the food you are eating. These are ways to begin your day in a calm and peaceful way. Take time to say a prayer of gratitude and to set an intention for the day. If you have a commute to work, play peaceful music, make up prayerful songs, or sing along with recorded life-affirming songs. All of these are tools that can help you center yourself first thing in the morning. The feelings engendered by centering allow you to create a health-giving, prayerful, and balanced foundation from which your day can be built.

   If you have children or a partner, take the time to smile at them and wish them a good day. A hug and a kiss go a long way into a new day.

2. Morning Invocation

> Mother Crystal,
> Deep in the Earth
> Waiting
> I call on you.
> My heart is open.
> I call on you.
>
> Golden Eagle,
> High in the Heavens
> Soaring
> I call on you.
> My heart is open.
> I call on you.
>
> Red-tailed Hawk,
> In the East
> Illuminating
> I call on you.
> My Heart is open.
> I call on you.
>
> Hummingbird,
> In the South
> Connecting
> I call on you.
> My Heart is open.
> I call on you.
>
> Snake,
> In the West
> Deepening
> I call on you.
> My heart is open.
> I call on you.

Bear,
In the North
Purifying
I call on you.
My heart is open.
I call on you.

Great Spirit,
You are everywhere
Loving
I call on you.
You are my heart.
I am loving you.

3. Cherokee Morning Ritual

While I attended the Unity Council gatherings in Tennessee, I was taught a beautiful morning ritual done for centuries by the Cherokee people. This is how it was told to me: "Our habit was to 'go to water' first thing in the morning, in order to sing praises to the rising sun, cleanse ourselves, and begin the new day with a clean body, open heart, clear mind. In this manner, we acknowledged of our gratitude for our connection to *all there is*. We went to the river singing a sacred morning song. Standing at the edge, we brought water six times to the crown and the seventh time to the heart. A prayer of gratitude was made and an intention set for the day. In the old days, a refreshing plunge was made into the cold clear river."

Sadly, not many of us live near a river or one that is clean enough to bathe in. Instead, you might sing a favorite hymn that affirms all of life, learn a sacred song that appeals to you, or make one up that honors the sun and a new beginning. You might sing in the shower every morning as you touch the water six times to your crown and a seventh to your heart. You could say a prayer and think about how you want to move through the day, saying these things out loud. When you come out of the front door of your residence on your way to work, you might stop at a special little altar that you have created. As you touch the earth at the bottom of your steps, or greet her at your altar, offer her kind words, a song, cornmeal, or tobacco, and tell her how much you appreciate the abundance that she provides in your life. This altar could be made up of some special flowers and stones or other treasures you have collected from walks while enjoying nature and earth's abundance. If you live in the city, your altar should be located right inside your front door or in the hallway if it is safe. Photographs of favorite places, treasures collected from travels, or fresh flowers from the corner market could be a part of this altar.

Find a way to stop and bring into your conscious awareness the love that you feel for yourself, for the sun, for the earth, for God, for all of the animals, birds, the special people in your life, and for all that feeds you and nourishes you. Have fun creating rituals that strengthen your day and acknowledge the cycle of the moon and the season of the year. Invite friends to do them with you. Every day, make time to honor the sacred in your life.

4. God Has Stopped

"Everything as it moves,
now and then, here and there,
makes stops.
The bird as it flies stops in one place to make its nest,
and in another to rest in its flight.
A man when he goes forth stops when he wills.
So the god has stopped.
The sun, which is so bright and beautiful,
is one place where he has stopped.
The moon, the stars, the winds, he has been with.
The trees, the animals, are all where he has stopped,
and the Indian thinks of these places and sends prayers there
to reach the place where the god has stopped
and win help and a blessing."

—Anonymous Dakota Sioux wise man[33]

5. Early Morning Meditations

Three Women at Sunrise
The sky blazes with reds and oranges
Caught in the underbelly of clouds
Turning to yellows and golds
Framed by grays and blues.
Light spills out
along the undulating surface of the water
Filling the world with color and tone.

The light show continues for a long time
While three women wait patiently for the sun to come.

---

[33]   T. C. McLuhan, *Touch the Earth* (Simon and Schuster, 1972), p.37.

Songs are sung
Prayers are made
Gratitude is expressed.

Then
One woman seeks treasures along the shore
As beauty stretches out before her.

Another jumps into the belly of the ocean
Held and rocked by the gentle rise and fall of the Mother.

The third struggles
Wanting to be in both places at once.
She sits
Focusing on the treasures inside
And finds the sun rising in her heart.

I sit on the picnic table on the deck looking out over the ocean, blanket folded underneath me, another wrapped around my shoulders. The chilly predawn air greets my nostrils as I breathe deeply in and out of my body.

As the breathing subsides to hardly noticeable, I begin to focus my awareness in my heart then slowly slide it down my spine, extending through my belly and root to deep into the earth. I take the time to establish a good strong connection, breathing it alive, before moving back into my heart. From the heart, I move my awareness upward through my throat to the pituitary and pineal glands to the crown and then upward to the heavens.

The sensation of my body grows long and stretched.

I make a conscious connection with my ancestors who have come before me, those who have prayed for me. They sit behind me and are accompanied by the line of light of my spiritual ancestral heritage. I am grateful for these beings of light, who guide my spiritual growth and development and who understand my place in the bigger picture. This line of light stretches before me and includes those generations who will come after me and for whom I pray.

I connect to the teachers, who have had an important impact on my life.

I picture each one and offer my gratitude.

I touch into the morphogenic field of Native American spirituality and the Naraya. I give thanks for the rich experiences I have been given.

I open to the team of spiritual beings who work with me and give thanks for all of the joy that they bring and all of the lessons that they teach me.

Focusing back on my experience, I feel a strong, warm, loving sensation in my heart. My body has lost its density. I feel very big with no boundaries except

LIVING LIFE AS A PRAYER

for a strong sensation in my heart. It is as if this center of consciousness is all that is left of my personal self.

If I choose, I can focus my attention on another person or another thing by focusing my awareness and leaning my energy in that direction. There is a sense of a huge glob of amorphic substance (thick but not dense, liquid and flowing, not solid) that extends, flows from my center in the direction of the other. As our energies merge, I can feel into this other and know their experience as a sensation of texture and energy.

As I connect with my root and light center above my crown and connect heart center with half-opened, defocused eyes, the intense sensation of light on the inside becomes an experience of light on the outside. The ocean glows, edges are soft and luminous, less and less solid.

Closing my eyes again, I experience luminous clouds of electric blue/purple, sometimes moving in decreasing irregular concentric circles or spirals toward an invisible center point. I seem to be in space, floating and connected to my body at the same time. The connection is to an undulating spark of blue light that feels like it is the center of my consciousness. There are a myriad of other sparks in this vast sea of space that are like the stars and galaxies. The inner and outer seem one and the same. I have no sense of time or my physical presence, only a place from which I am conscious of all that is unfolding. I rest here, deeply filled.

Opening my eyes slowly, I become aware of the sound of undulating waves breaking on the shore. The starlit sky is beginning to fade. The black gray ocean takes shape and changes to lighter shades of gray, green, and dark blue.

Sun Love
Early in the morning
I sit and wait
Wondering
How and when my lover will come.

A huge dark mushroom cloud
Obscures the path.
Will he come this morning?

Teasing
His colors begin to show
Subtle at first
As if he's tickling my fancy.

"I'm here," he says
Reaching out
With mauves, pinks, and harvest straw
Inviting.

Enjoying his cleverness
Intrigued
I breathe slow and deep
Expanded
Edges loosened
Opening
Feeling the fullness of my being.

Brilliant pinks
Begin to outline
The backs of clouds
Announcing his presence.

Gradually
Imperceptibly almost
The rim of pinks
Turn to liquid
Light comes alive.

The shapes of nearby clouds
Are pulled from flat to full
As edges are outlined
With pink and gold.

Intensified
The rim of living yellow
Is accompanied by
Small clouds
Once invisible
Dancing a puffy golden dance.

The drama
The tease
The waiting
I feel myself rising to the call.

As the sky above
Begins to glow
An orange gold
Light streams forth into the heavens

He's almost here!
Anticipating
The magnificence of his presence
My body begins to shudder.

As He bursts forth
Over the rim of liquid yellow
Love rocks my body
Pulls my breath up short
Fills me with bliss.

Sweetly
He extends
A path of undulating golden light
To the door of my heart.

6. Opening Your Morning to the Divine

1. Beginning the day in a prayerful manner sets a positive tone for the rest of the day.
2. Take time to meditate, set an intention, and organize/prioritize your day.
3. Develop a morning ritual that puts you in touch with the Divine within and without.
4. Set up an altar to honor the earth and recognize the beauty and abundance in your life. Stop there on your way out the door to pray and feel the *divine love* that you carry in your heart.
5. Go slowly and thoughtfully into the day. Notice where God has stopped. Send prayers and a blessing.
6. Embrace ecstasy at every possible moment.

CHAPTER VII

Embracing Abundance

Mother, Father, God, Universal Power
Remind us daily of the sanctity of all life.
Touch our Hearts with the glorious oneness
of all of creation,
As we strive to respect all the living beings
on this planet.
Penetrate our souls with the beauty of this
earth,
As we attune ourselves to the rhythm and
flow of the seasons.
Awaken our minds with the knowledge to
achieve a world in perfect harmony
And grant us the wisdom to realize that we
can have heaven on earth.

Jo Poore[34]

1. Abundance

The time has come to give up the old model of fear and scarcity, which states, "I am never good enough." "I never have enough." "I don't deserve to take up space in this body." This model says that we can never measure up and that we always need to buy more. Our consumer society has taught us to "shop 'til we drop," to use and throw away, and to spend beyond our means. We experience a hunger that becomes impossible to fill. This model has produced a culture that rapes and pillages the earth, without thought, demanding more and more of her resources and products. "Progress is our most important product" is a phrase I grew up with. This belief has resulted in an environmental crisis of monumental proportions.

Back in 1854, Chief Seattle warned the newly arrived commissioner of Indian Affairs for the Washington Territory, "Continue to contaminate your bed and

---

[34]   Roberts, *Earth Prayers*, p. 179.

you will, one night, suffocate in your own waste." He urged, "The white man does not seem to notice the air he breathes. Like a man dying for many days, he is numb to the stench. But if we sell you our land, you must remember that the air is precious to us, that the air shares its spirit with all the life it supports. The wind that gave our grandfather his first breath also receives his last sigh. And the wind must also give our children the spirit of life. And if we sell you our land, you must keep it apart and sacred, as a place where even the white man can go to taste the wind that is sweetened by the meadow's flowers."

Among those who are working on the front lines to remind us that we must consider our environment is my youngest son, Marin Goldstein. He writes in December of 1998, "On a misty morning in February, as we lead a group of Buddhists into the heart of the Headwaters Redwood Forest (California), the experience of hope was tangible in the air. They had been given a special vase, which was made in Nepal from clay and the ground bones of ancient Tibetan lamas, to take into the forest. They were to create a sacred space and bury it. This vase and its contents were to emanate a promise of love and compassion to all the species living on our Earth Mother.

"As the day unfolded, the mists drew apart and the sun shone on the muddy logging roads, which left scars deep into the hillsides. Crossing the rushing torrents of sweet springs and entering the magical lands of the heart of the forest, our sense of mission grew. As we walked among the great trees standing so tall and proud, we knew we must hold the vision. Bowing our heads under the decaying bodies of these giants that crossed our trail, we beheld a promise of new beginnings. When these mighty redwood beings die, their bodies continue to serve to fertilize the littlest of forest flowers and brilliant redwood sorrel.

"In the confluence of two raging mountain streams hidden beneath forest decay, we were drawn to the foot of one great tree. It wasn't particularly special in a forest of spectacular trees. It wasn't even the oldest among trees that grow beyond two thousand years in age, but it promised to hold the space sacred that we created at its feet.

"We offered this vessel, which carried the hopes and dreams from people of ancient times to modern, from people across the globe to those close at hand living in the Green Gulch Zen community, and from activists of the Headwaters Forest community. Placed in the body of the vase were precious gifts from the heart: precious gems, drops of human blood, stones, and feathers. Even though to the eyes of corporate America, these gifts were meaningless, to us they were gifts of courage and vision that overflowed from our hearts.

"Accompanied by the chanting of Buddhist sutras, we dug deep into the richest and most fertile soil my fingers have ever touched. This soil contains the stories of life and death for more time than the entire human species could tell. Reaching down into its promise of life, we buried that vessel. The vibrations of our shared visions were left to spread outward from the heart of this great forest.

"There are many other vessels of this sort that are being buried across our planet. As our strength grows and our courage broadens, these vibrations will touch the hearts of all of our Earth Mother's creations."

In order to shift our relationship with the earth and all of life, we need to release fear and scarcity and embrace abundance. Instead of focusing on negativity and chaos and feeling like we are either victims or perpetrators, we can learn to take a deep breath, feel the quiet strength of our own center, and affirm our deep relationship to the Divine. Embracing abundance can be as simple as smelling the spring meadow flowers on the wind, as Chief Seattle encourages us to do, or touching the soil at the base of a giant redwood. Embracing abundance can mean that we stop buying the latest toys and that we be content with ourselves and the fullness of life all around us. To recognize the vast beauty found in the smallest flower, to be aware of the way in which we use the resources available to us brings us to an awareness of the abundant nature of the earth. This radiant living being needs to be taken into account and a partnership developed with her.

Let us learn to create a sustainable environment, so that there will be beautifully clear sparkling rivers filled with fish and other marine life for years to come. Our children and the many generations to follow will need good water to drink, fresh air to breathe, and healthy soil to produce healthy food.

Stop and think before you cut down that tree in your yard or order old growth redwood trim for your deck. Ask the spirits of your land if cutting the tree will serve the total environment of your land. Learn to work in partnership with nature, who always helps us keep the health of the total environment in mind.

Machaelle Small Wright gives us a method for developing a partnership with nature in her book, *Co-Creative Science*.[35] If you must build another house or office building, explore methods that work with the environment. Using solar—or wind-based electrical power, building with straw or recycled materials, experimenting with composting toilets and other alternative earth-friendly construction techniques are some exciting ways to explore living with the earth instead of against her.

The resources on this planet are not endless. The aquifers created thousands of years ago continue to bring us water. But for how much longer will they? More and more, we dip greedy straws into the pool to drink without thinking of the consequences. Desperately, we need to recognize what we do have, honor the resources available to us, and use them wisely. We cannot wait any longer for just one more house to be built and one more tree to be cut down in a way

---

[35] Machelle Small Wright, *Co-Creative Science: A Revolution in Science Providing Real Solutions for Today's Health and Environment* (Virginia: Perelandra, Ltd., 1998).

that does not support the environment. Let us create sustainable lives for our planet and ourselves and protect the beauty we treasure for our children and our children's children. Embracing abundance means acknowledging the beauty that is already all around us and developing a partnership with nature to bring about heaven on earth.

2. Experiencing the Abundant Universe

The Beloved,
pressing close,
smiling sweetly,
discovers the chimes
hanging in the window
of my heart,
resonating.

A dear young friend, who just finished nursing school, was told that she had the highest grade-point average in her class. At Women's Circle,[36] she shared that she had been taken by surprise because it was not something that she had been striving for. All of a sudden, she felt the pressure to get a high grade on the last test.

For this last test, she did everything she had taught herself how to do. Before, when she studied in preparation for the test, and again, when she was actually taking the test, she centered herself and opened a coning to ask her test-taking team for assistance. This team was made up of the Overlighting Deva of human healing, nature, the academic aspect of the White Brotherhood, her higher self, the deva of the subject matter she was studying, and the deva of the specific test to be given on such and such a date. She focused their combined energies on the task at hand by explaining in detail what it was that she needed. She got a very good grade. This time, the process felt awful, she had added a new component. She was no longer within the flow of energy because she was self-conscious and working hard to achieve a high grade. It was painful. This time, she felt pressured, off center, tired, and grumpy. Before, when the high grade hadn't been the driving force, she finished studying and test-taking feeling joyous and energized.

At this Women's Circle, she also questioned whether she deserved the rewards that were coming to her at graduation. Through the course of her study, she had learned to be within the flow so easily that the information she needed came quickly. She saw her other classmates struggle long and hard to do the

---

[36] I started holding Women's Circles in 1993. We met monthly to pray, sing, dance, and share our journeys in order to develop a supportive community.

work. Was it right that she should get the reward when the process had been so much fun?

When she began nursing school, she and her very active young son were living with me. I watched her work hard to balance time and energy between being a good mother and a good student. I watched her stay up late into the night after he was asleep, in order to thoroughly go over the material for the next day's test. Slowly, as she learned to draw in help from spirit guides and helpers, the process became easier and easier. She was no longer struggling hard to do the work but began to learn how to ride the currents of knowledge by being present to herself and connecting with the help available to her.

We have a work ethic that says, "No pain, no gain." Is that why she doesn't deserve the graduation rewards, because she learned how not to suffer through the process? Instead, she really loved her work and joyfully moved through the process of learning what she would need to know to be a good nurse. Are we still waiting for our reward in heaven that will come only if we work hard and suffer from day to day in this life? What loving God would want such a thing? What about the possibility of co-creating (working cooperatively with God to create) heaven on earth through a daily practice of being present to the joy and beauty of all of life?

As students in Earth School, we are learning to live life with conscious awareness. If we open our hearts to the Divine within ourselves, we can learn to feed ourselves and those around us the love we find. By attending Earth School, we benefit from the lessons our souls receive from being in physical form. Being in a physical form means that we can experience life from three different perspectives that are united into one. We have a body, a mind, and spirit. Each one of these perspectives is different and not separate from the whole of who we are. We gather information through the use of our sensory system: seeing, hearing, touching, tasting, smelling, and feeling. And we are learning to expand to other ways of knowing.

How might we move from a scarcity model filled with fear and negativity to a model that notices the beauty that is present in our lives right now? This model of abundance sees what is already present and unfolding just as it should be. It says that each of us is beautiful, inside and out. It acknowledges the good food on the table, the friendships that surround us, the good music on the stereo, the loving animals on your lap, and the soft gentle spring rain falling outside, which nourishes the Mother Earth. It means that we need to take the time to see the bright primroses in the garden and the beautiful red cardinal sitting in the holly tree with its red berries and glossy green leaves. We can choose to notice our good health, the feeling of love, and the good energy flowing through our bodies. Slowing down and relaxing our minds helps us to stop and appreciate all of the abundance that is everywhere . . . only waiting to be noticed.

The abundance model, which focuses on the positive aspects of what already exists, shifts our perspectives both internally and externally. Internally, we focus on our strengths and on our ability to learn. Mistakes are not failures but are opportunities to learn how we might shift our awareness to create a different outcome. Initially, we begin to look at who we are. What can we contribute as individuals and communities to the greater whole? Externally, we begin to notice the beauty that is around us. As we learn to appreciate the inherent balance in nature, we learn not to act as individuals imposing our will on others and the environment, but as part of a co-creative partnership with nature in order to create balance and harmony together.

In a time of severe drought, we hadn't had much rain to speak of in almost a year. The lush woods of southern Maryland are born from rainy springs and hot humid summers. It was hard to see the trees come slow to leaf and then droop for lack of water. Plants in the garden matured very quickly, as if fulfilling their reproductive cycle was imperative for the survival of their species.

Neighbors seemed oblivious to the preciousness of water. They ritually watered their lawns, not in August, as usual, but in May and June. I mentioned concern over the level of water in the aquifer to someone, who replied that he was on city water so he didn't have to worry. I found it odd that we are so distant from the source of the things, and we have come to take so much for granted. I was saving my bath water in order to water a few plants, and I was taking fewer and fewer baths. I was grateful for the straw mulch, which was holding some of the moisture in the soil next to the roots of my vegetable plants.

As a gardener and as an observer of nature, I felt deeply the stress of the plants and animals. The earth was thirsty. Meanwhile, my sister, who lives in Seattle, reported that it hadn't stopped raining for four months. In some places in our country, the rivers were at record heights; while in others, they were at record lows. There were so many imbalances.

I sang to the rising sun in the morning, thanking it for its warmth, light, energy, strength, and beauty. Without the sun, we would be a cold stone flying out of control in space. The drought found me saying a "yes, but" kind of prayer. "Yes, thank you for your bright shining face, but where are the clouds filled with the rain we so desperately need?" I talk to my clients all the time about making "yes, but" statements. The "but" completely wipes away the first part of the sentence, so in effect, I was not acknowledging the sun. Here I was, dismissing it.

Recognizing what I was doing, I realized that I needed to shift my attention to the beauty that was all around me in spite of the chaos. When I spent my time worrying about the trees, plants, and animals, I was putting out negative energy. When I focused on the dryness, the wilting of the plants, and the lack of blossoms on the mountain laurel, I moved into a pattern of worry that carried me round and round like a dog chasing its tail. This negative energy was depleting mine, carrying me to a place of hopelessness and despair, which was neither very useful nor even very helpful. And I certainly didn't feel good. Instead, when I gave thanks for the beautiful bright clear sunny day, the joyous breeze, the beauty of the flowers, vegetables, and trees that were continuing on in the bright warmth of the sun, I basked in the feelings of love and joy. These were the feelings that I could then bring not only to myself but also to the world around me.

So I learned to take time to notice what was happening. I watered a few plants, kept the birdbaths and feeders full, and didn't flush the toilets as much. I was now free to focus lots of positive energy on the beauty that continued to sustain me. It was interesting to balance the knowledge of what was and take actions based on love, by not slipping into negativity or denial.

The abundance model led me to a feeling of partnership and contentment. Feelings of abundance can create a sense of community working together to create a powerful life-affirming team. When we perceive everyone and everything as having a valuable contribution to make to the greater good of the whole, we acknowledge that all aspects of creation are interdependent. A feeling of respect, love, peace, and beauty emerge from this way of being. I had fun writing the following poem.

The Stream
As summer moved along,
I had to tighten my belt
and watch those clouds
come and go
without a drop
left over for me.

THEN THE STORM CAME
blowing through,
and like a wild child
suddenly set free and loose,
I danced in all my glory.
Moving this way and that,
I ran through those woods.

Now that my belly's full,
gurgling with contentment,
I laze my way through
new cut paths
and old familiar ones,
admiring the sand
I laid high up on
the forest floor.

3. A Navaho Prayer

"Eastern Mountain, Chief of all Mountains, I walk
with your feet, I walk with your legs, I walk with your body
and with your sound.
The feathers on your head I walk with;
they are in front of me, beautiful; under me, beautiful;
on top of me, beautiful.
Oh, Mountain of the East, I am the one
that lives on forever.
Everything is beautiful.
Everything is beautiful.
Out of my mouth, beauty, and around me beauty.
I AM EVERLASTING MAN!
Around me everything is beautiful.
Around me everything is beautiful.
Around me everything is beautiful.

Jeff King, Navajo Chantways Singer[37]

4. Embracing Beauty

Join me as I let my breath slowly all of the way out and easily fill my lungs
with a nice long deep breath. Paying a great deal of attention to my breathing,
I feel the continuous flow of in-breath and out-breath as it moves in and out of
my body. I imagine that my breath and my energy are like a figure eight, the
sign for infinity with my heart as its center. I see one loop emanating from my
heart, stretching high above my head into the heavens, while the opposite loop
reaches into the earth below me. Each loop of the figure eight is being
created with each out-breath and in-breath. Slowly releasing my breath, I imagine
sending a line of energy stretching out from my heart into the heavens above.
As I begin to draw the air in, I feel that line of energy gathering in the energy
from above as it curves around and loops back into my heart. As I release the
next breath, I watch the line of energy emanating from my heart reaching deep
down into the earth below my feet. As the line begins to curve around and shift
to inhaling long and slow, I feel the energy of the earth being gathered up and
moving back into my heart. As I continue to breathe deeply, I feel the loops of
energy bringing love from the earth and the heavens into my heart. With each
flow of breath outward, I give my love back to the earth and the heavens. I see
this figure eight of sparkling light flowing between us like a river looping back

---

[37] *Navajo: Walk in Beauty*, p. 57.

and forth. I am aware that as the breath moves back into my body, I feel love being returned to me over and over. I understand that there is an infinite supply of love flowing between my heart and the heart of the universe. I feel full and beautiful. "My cup runneth over."

I continue to experience the same in-flow and out-flow of breath and love. And this time, I imagine that I can see the loop stretch out in front of me and behind me, to the right side of me and to the left side of me. I draw in loving energy from the world around me and give back all of the love that I have.

My breathing is initiating a continuous exchange of sparkling light and love that moves back and forth between myself and all of life. I immerse myself in the love and beauty that comes from me and is given back to me. I become the flowing river of light and love.

I find myself dreaming about living in heaven on earth. Placing my dream in the middle of all of creation and breathing loving energy into it, I feel the response coming back. I know that world peace begins at home in my own heart and that I have the opportunity to live that reality. I am one with all of creation and we are beautiful from the inside out and the outside in.

5. A Small Piece of Heaven on Earth

In the forest
moonlight cloaks me
nature spirits greet me
breathing coolness on my cheeks
draining away the day's weariness.

Dancing,
my feet
tap
the smooth, soft skin of the Mother.

Listening
beyond the sound of wind in leaves
beyond the sound of water falling in its bed,
I hear the stars singing,
feel the Earth praying,
smell manna hanging in the trees.

6. Scarcity vs. Abundance in Review

The scarcity model comes from the fears that arise from feeling like we will never measure up, never be good enough and never have enough. Our experience becomes polarized into victim vs. perpetrator. This model is fed by

156

our consumer society that requires buying more than we need and encourages the creation of debt. Progress in this model demands domination over the earth and promotes an attitude of entitlement to all of her resources. The feeling of scarcity results in our fascination with crisis and traumas that are continually made visible to us through the newspapers, the television, and the movies. We can easily become swallowed up in a world of negativity and unhappiness.

The abundance model teaches us to focus on the beauty and the positive forces available to us in what already exists. We learn to believe in ourselves, see our strengths, and learn to contribute the best of who we are to the greatest good of all of life. Mistakes are opportunities to learn more about who we are and to learn to expand our abilities to respond in more creative ways. The abundance model promotes partnership with each other, with our environment, the earth, and with the vast array of help available to us. We learn to seek solutions to problems by honoring and respecting the interconnectedness of all of life. Divine love is always available unconditionally.

CHAPTER VIII

Opening to Other Sources of Information

"In ancient time, an initiate, seeker, or person needing guidance would come before the elders. The elders were usually six in number and sat in the North. The elders were wise, not simply because they had led a long life, but because they knew the inner secrets. They understood the Wolf trails of the mind, experienced many powerful visions, and owned their powers and gifts . . . The need for this type of guidance exists today."

Jamie Sams[38]

1. Guidance

When I was pulling something out of the refrigerator for breakfast one Saturday morning, I noticed that the shelves were in need of being wiped down. One thing led to another, and before I knew it, I had taken everything out. When I realized that this job was going to take a while, I decided to turn off the refrigerator. After I had washed everything down thoroughly, chipped the extra ice out of the freezer, and replaced the food, I tried to turn it back on, but there was no response.

I turned the dial to the "off" position and back to "on" several times just to make sure. Still nothing. When in doubt, the saying goes, give it a sound thump on the side. So I tried that just in case something was loose somewhere. Still nothing. I checked to be sure that it was still plugged in and even went so far as to check the circuit breakers to see if one had mysteriously gone off by a mistake. Everything was fine there.

I decided to call for help, since I had exhausted my repertoire of solutions. When I asked for someone in the service department, the woman who answered the phone said she could probably answer almost any question I had. After I explained my dilemma, she suggested tapping the thermostat because, as she explained, "sometimes it sticks." I had to ask where the thermostat was. She

---

[38] Jamie Sams, *Medicine Cards* (Santa Fe: Bear and Company, 1988), p. 16.

directed me to the dial with the numbers inside on the back. I thanked her, hung up, and decided that my rolling pin was an appropriate tool for the job. I tapped cautiously. Nothing. I tapped a little more enthusiastically. Nothing. I waited, thinking that if I gave it a break, something might be different. Still nothing.

By this time, I was beginning to get a little upset, so I called her back. Could she please send someone out to fix the problem? "I'm sorry, but this is Saturday, and there are no service men here. Call back on Monday." All I could see was that the rest of the day would be spent cooking all of the food in my freezer in order to preserve it. That was not what I had planned to do for the day.

Then it occurred to me. If devas are light beings, who are responsible for bringing energy into form, then there must be a deva for the refrigerator. I decided to call on the deva of the refrigerator and see what would happen. My whole body shook with the incoming energy as the deva enthusiastically joined me, as if to say, "What took you so long to ask?" When I explained the problem, I asked if I should lay my hands on the refrigerator to jump-start it.

I was remembering the winter before, when the battery in my truck had given out halfway down my long hilly driveway. I had called the tow truck for help. He had tried a number of times unsuccessfully to get it started and had begun to make noises about towing it into the service station. Several thoughts had flashed through my mind at the same time: one, towing would cost more money than I had to spend at the moment; two, I really needed my truck for other things I had to do that day. I asked if he would try just one more time. I had no idea if this would work, but I placed my hands on the hood of the truck and imagined lightning bolts coming down into the engine. Much to my surprise, the truck started right up. I did end up needing a new battery, but I drove myself to the store to buy it. It sure beat the money and time required for being towed to the garage!

Unlike the deva of my truck, the deva of the refrigerator did not like the idea of a jump-start, so I began going down a list of possible solutions. Nothing I could think of was the proper solution. I was uncertain. What now? I told the deva I was really going to need some help because I couldn't think of anything else. Amazingly, the thought of a fox came immediately to mind. I actually had a fox skin in my freezer. It had been there for about three or four years. Soon after I had moved down to the county, I had come across a beautiful red fox that had just been hit. I don't usually stop for road kill, but he was so beautiful. I offered a pinch of tobacco as a gift in return for the fox and put him in the back of my truck. I decided that it was important for me to take responsibility for my actions and learn how to skin the animal myself. His pelt would make a beautiful sacred pipe bag. A friend came over, brought his tools, and we worked for most of the day. The job was not quite done when he had to leave, so I rolled up the remaining skin, telling myself I'd finish it soon. He had the tools, and I never got back to the task. The fox was still waiting for me in my freezer some four years later.

Apparently, the deva thought it would be a good idea if I took it out and buried the remains, giving the fox back to the Earth Mother. No sooner did I take that fox out of the freezer and close the door than the refrigerator started right up. I was awestruck.

One moral of the story is this: there is a lot of help available when you take the time to ask. Another might be, don't be outfoxed. Guidance can come in many different forms. All we really need to do is ask. It is important to be open to a myriad of possibilities. If I had kept a set of expectations about the way I would receive help, I might not have accepted the information in the form in which it arrived, because I would have been looking in another direction.

Another wonderful example comes from the book *Mutant Message Down Under*. The storyteller is being taken on a walkabout by a group of aboriginal people. They are walking though very hot and dry land and carrying only a little water with them. Each day, they say a prayer similar to the one at the beginning of this book. They pray to the Creator to be provided for, and each day, they find food. They had to be willing to eat a wide variety of things, but they never went hungry.

Marin tells the story of an encounter that took place with a deer while he was visiting his father in northern Vermont. "In the slanting light of the late afternoon, I watched from inside as a young deer walked into the field. Urged by a feeling inside not to sit idly by and watch, I walked out the backdoor and very slowly approached her. At first, she was simply grazing. She was alone against the backdrop of the swaying branches of the trees in the forest. As I silently entered into her space, she looked up. Her dark brown eyes connected intensely with my blue ones. In a fleeting shimmer of fear, I thought that the deer might run, but to my amazement, she walked directly toward me. Holding her head high and keeping eye contact, she came within ten feet of where I was standing. I didn't dare move and could not help but smile. She was very beautiful. Her gown of soft brown fur was tipped with white snow. It felt as if her deep brown eyes engulfed my soul. She had a smartness about her as she cocked her head sniffing to the right and to the left. For my part, I felt frozen in space, hardly breathing. My stillness only seemed to cause her to lose interest.

"Walking to my right and taking her eyes from me only in brief moments at a time, she softly nibbled on the leaves of the apple tree. In order to relieve my frozen aching body, I succumbed to slightly shifting my weight. She took notice immediately and watched intently. I couldn't help but laugh. Her curiosity and my feeble attempts at silence must have been a match to watch. As we both eased into this unusual experience, she slowly moved toward me as I knelt down in front of her. Although she wouldn't take the grass I offered her, she brushed her wet nose up against my fingers in appreciation.

"Apparently, much to my amazement, she thought I was an unusual deer to play with, for she laid her front legs low and bucked up into the air. My immediate reaction was not as open. I thought, 'Shit! What now?' Taken aback by her jumping and bucking, I made up the excuse that it must be time for supper and I needed to get back to the cabin. At first, dumbfounded by my reaction, she watched me go and then began to follow. She was twenty feet away when I entered the cabin.

"I have to confess that I breathed a great sigh of relief. This amazing experience was so utterly beyond words. In just a moment, however, my feelings shifted. I missed her. I looked outside to see her grazing again as if she was waiting for my return. Maybe she knew somehow that I needed that moment of comfortable reality to check in and reorient myself. Taking a few deep breaths, I walked back outside.

"Over the next three hours, I played with this gentle creature, who was so completely full of life. She continued to play her jumping game, expecting me to join in. She seemed to laugh with me as I chose to simply watch. I was intrigued and wished that I had been in a better frame of mind to have engaged with her in that game. Still, we played in the tall grass and short grass, walked along the forest edge, and ate our food together. One special moment occurred when she trusted me enough to get up on her hind legs and nibble the tender birch leaves right in front of me. Because I am tall, I could reach up and grab the branch. I held it down for her so that she could eat to her heart's content without using the extra energy it took to stand on just two legs. This sense of cooperation made me feel ecstatic.

"As the shadows of night lengthened, the time to part came. I prayed with her, hoping in the future she wouldn't mistake other dangerous human scents with my loving human heart and end up being killed by some lusty hunter. I promised her sacred space on the land and hoped to see her again. My father, who had stayed in the cabin the whole time, said she came to the glade for several days waiting to see if I would return. It was strange to leave after such a brief moment of deep connection. This was such a profound sharing beyond the limitations of language and species.

"As my future unfolds before me, the deer reminds me to stay in the present moment, pay attention to life's surprises and enjoy them."

An old adage says, "Be careful of what you ask for, because you might just get it." You have to be willing to take responsibility for the answers you receive. If you pray for guidance and receive an answer, you have to be willing to accept it and not say, "Sorry, I don't like the response, so I'll ask again and see if I get another answer I like better." At the same time, we have all been given free will, so we can choose to say no.

Do you remember the story about the man who was on the roof of his house, surrounded by water? He was praying for God to save him from the flood. First, a man came floating by on a log and offered him a ride. Second, a man came in a boat, and third, another man arrived in a helicopter. Each time, the man said no because he was waiting for God to show up and save him. After he had drowned and was standing at the pearly gates, he asked God why he had let him down. God said, "I sent you a log, a boat, and a helicopter. What more did you want?"

A number of years ago, when I was considering whether or not to go to graduate school in psychology, I went to consult a psychic about that and some other issues in my life at the time. When I asked the graduate-school question, she said it wouldn't really make a difference because I was to go to Washington, D.C., and do something important for the brotherhood and sisterhood. Oh my, I thought, I'm going to go into politics. I had been recently elected in the state of Vermont to attend the first National Women's Convention in Houston, Texas. This had been a wonderful experience, but I had no political aspirations. I chose to go to graduate school anyway. I continue to be very grateful for that choice, because being a psychologist brings me great joy. I forgot about the D.C. part until years later, when I was living just north of that city. I had been considerably in debt after graduate school and my ensuing postdoctoral internship with the Los Angeles Police Department. I had taken the first job offer with the Montgomery County Police Department, just north of Washington, D.C. Curious!

There is also such a thing as right timing. We may not be ready to handle what we are asking for, and we may need some other steps to happen first. As I have mentioned before, I used to be a very speedy person. I wanted everything to have happened yesterday. An important lesson for me has been to learn to honor my own process and slow down so I could pay attention to the answers that are readily available.

As in the birthing process, our bodies know exactly what to do. We simply need to learn to get out of our own way. That means getting our own egos out of the way. Our egos offer us self-imposed limits, set patterns of behavior, expectations, as well as an important sense of who we are in the world. This sense sometimes needs to change, to accommodate a bigger sense of who we are. Often, prayers in the Sweat Lodge are framed with the phrase, "Creator, give us what we need, but no more than we can handle."

Another rule of thumb when praying is to ask for something specific, not something broad and general. Rather than ask for a healing, ask specifically for what you wish to heal. If I feel myself coming down with the stomach flu that has been going around, I name the specific symptoms that I am aware of and ask for help with work on those symptoms. If my knee is also bothering, but I don't mention it, chances are when the healing work is complete, my knee will still be bothering me. I didn't ask for help with it, so I will need to address that in a separate prayer.

There are many unseen intelligences that are more than willing to work with us. They only wait for us to ask for help. My experience is that those who accompany us are asking to work with us in co-creative partnerships in a very loving way to bring about the highest good for all concerned. They will only work within our set intention and will never override our free will to make choices.

Medicine helpers, like a bird, animal, plant, or reptile, show themselves to us in very out of the ordinary ways, like Marin's deer or my snake. They usually come to work with us in special ways. They may carry a special message or teaching or help with a healing. Jamie Sams instructs us, "When you call upon the power of an animal, you are asking to be drawn into complete harmony with the strength of that creature's essence. Gaining understanding from these brothers and sisters of the animal kingdom is a healing process, and must be approached with humility and intuitiveness."[39]

Hummingbirds have been moving powerfully in and out of my life ever since my first *vision quest* when I spent the night on a hill alone under the stars. I was seeking a vision that would help me understand how I could best serve the people. My altar space was a small area that was marked off in each of the four directions by poles around which four hundred prayer ties (small red, yellow, white, and black cloth pouches of tobacco) were strung. The poles were decorated with eagle feathers and tobacco tied into strips of colored cloth.

During the night, I danced and sang to the insistent rhythm of the whippoorwill. People from our community came periodically with Sings Alone, the medicine man who was responsible for me, to sing the familiar Lakota songs. They would sing one song, and I would return with another. Three times we would take our turns. I could not see them, or they me, but this was the way the community showed their support to me and checked up on my welfare. I truly came to understand that praying for a vision was not for myself alone. I was part of a community of people, and the vision I was seeking would, in turn, serve that particular community, as well as the larger community.

The group of people, who gathered together weekly to take part in the Sweat Lodge purification ceremony, had taken time out of their busy lives to put me on the hill. One of the community members was spending the night in the Sweat Lodge on my behalf, praying for my safety and praying that a vision would come to me. The *vision quest* was not something that I could do alone. Sings Alone played a very important role by holding me in a protected sacred space and keeping a constant vigil. All of this was done with the help of his spirit guide and medicine helpers, because he was five miles away from where I was staying without food and water.

Midmorning the next day, wrapped in a wool blanket, I was holding my sacred pipe and praying quietly. A beautiful female ruby-throated hummingbird came and sat on the South Pole for a long time. I had never seen one so close and so still.

---

[39]   Sams, p. 13.

When I was brought down off of the hill, the community welcomed me with the greeting song, but no one was allowed to look at me. At that time, I was a sacred being. I was taken directly to the Sweat Lodge, where the last two rounds of the ceremony were performed. When it came time to smoke my pipe, I told Sings Alone every detail of my experience. After deep consultation with his spirit guide, he talked to me about what he understood. Hummingbird had come to offer herself as a medicine helper and would serve as a messenger from the people. I was deeply moved and very grateful that this beautiful little being had come to help me.

Several years later, I found myself sobbing uncontrollably when two friends revealed a pair of dead hummingbirds to a group of us who had come to a Unity Council gathering of the Cherokee people. Perfectly preserved, the female was sitting on the nest while the male was clutching the side of it. My friends had discovered the pair while climbing cliffs at Chaco Canyon in New Mexico. Long ago, the Anasasi people had settled here in the middle of the desert, built an enormous trading center, and perfectly constructed dwellings of desert stone. This civilization had flourished for several thousand years and then mysteriously disappeared. The intense emotion I felt at the sight of this beautiful yet pitiful pair and the mystery of the people inspired me to make plans to visit the site the next spring. I was sure I had something important to learn from this place. The hummingbirds were calling me to pay attention.

Just before winter solstice that same year, I had a dream that the Sweat Lodge community had gathered for a feast. I felt compelled to go outside and see the beautiful rosy colors of the sunrise. When I walked into the field, I saw a hummingbird. I was worried because it was late fall, and I was afraid that it would not find enough food. As I took a closer look, I discovered that it was unlike any hummingbird I had ever seen. It was larger and brilliant orange with a tinge of yellow along its wings and on the back of its head. It was so beautiful that I was mesmerized. In a very friendly manner, it began to fly fearlessly around me. In the dream state, I was thinking that this was not so strange, because the hummingbird was my medicine. Flying into my hair and face, it played with me and even let me hold it on my finger. The hummingbird came even closer and began to peck at a scab I apparently had on my forehead. At first, I was a little uncomfortable with this, but I began to think that perhaps I was giving it food.

The hummingbird flew even closer around my heart. At the same time, it was getting bigger and furrier. This became a very sensual and pleasurable experience. All of a sudden, I felt scared because I realized it was becoming part of me. As it merged with me, I tried to push it away, but it was too late. When the bird actually settled inside of me, I felt a sigh of relief because it felt wonderful. Soon, I was giggling and flitting around joyfully. I had become a hummingbird.

After the spring gathering of the Good Medicine Society in Arkansas, Marin and my partner at the time, Ed, and I headed out to the southwest to explore the Anasasi ruins at Chaco Canyon. We arrived in this magical place after turning off the main highway and winding for many miles down a long, rough dirt road. We set up camp just ahead of the summer solstice where a beautiful yellow meadowlark came every morning at dawn to serenade us awake. With the two ears of blue Anasasi corn that had been given to me, I wanted to go to the biggest kiva at sunrise to pray and meditate. I was sure that I would have a vision in this powerful place. I sat quietly within the circular enclosure waiting, for it was here long ago that the Anasasi priests performed their rituals to preserve the fragile balance of life-giving forces of nature. The positioning of certain windows marked the exact time of the summer solstice as the morning light streamed through them. While the starry night broke slowly into light and the great sun crested the surrounding cliffs, I waited. I felt nothing. It surprised me to feel so little energy in this ancient sacred site. I was disappointed, for I had been given no great vision as I had expected.

On the day we were scheduled to leave, we went hiking along the cliffs that rose up behind Pueblo Bonito, the largest of the building sites. We walked along the rim of the canyon past beautiful cactuses in bloom out across the desert to a small pueblo. The sky was vast, and the earth was beautiful. Here, there was such a different relationship between the two than back east where the earth seems to dominate.

When we came to a small circle of stones that marked the site of an ancient kiva, Ed offhandedly said to me, "That's where you are supposed to sit." So, I took my place in the center of the circle. Before I knew it, the whole world opened up to me. It was an experience that is difficult to express in words. It was as if I knew all beyond all knowing, could see beyond all horizons of seeing, was deep within the Divine, and connected to all of life. I have no idea how long I sat there, for time did not exist. Finally, humbly and quietly, I walked back to the truck.

We made one last stop at the Visitors Center before we left. My friends from the Unity Council had mentioned that they had found the birds in the cliffs behind the buildings, so I decided to check them out. What had seemed at the time to be a clear description of where they had been found was confusing when I was actually there, but I kept on walking back toward the cliffs. After a while, I looked up and gasped, for there on the face of one of the cliffs were the shadows of two hummingbirds with their beaks touching and wings outspread. There was no mistaking that the spirit of those two birds was still very present among the stones.

Later that summer, I built a Native American frame drum. I had received some guidance from the Council of ADRON that I needed to make a drum and go out into the woods and find out who I was. This felt imperative, and making the drum felt more like giving birth to myself. I painted the two ears of Anasasi corn, eagle feathers, and the vision of the two hummingbirds I had seen in Chaco Canyon on my drum. This was done to honor the profound experience I had had and to ask Hummingbird to guide my rebirth.

   Then, I began to take my drum and go for several days a month into the woods on a retreat. My moon time (menstrual) cycles were beginning to get very irregular. Desperately, I needed a regular anchor point with the earth and the moon because I could no longer find it in my body. With the help of my drum, the hummingbirds and long periods of quiet, I honored this transition and began to forge a new way of being.

   Nature and all my relatives (all aspects of creation) with whom I share this planet continue to be my biggest teachers.

   My friend Ellen and I decided to raise bees. I had been inspired by the Melissa in Starhawk's *The Fifth Sacred Thing.*[40] I had consulted the Overlighting Deva of this property to be sure that bringing bees into this environment would enhance and not detract from the integrity of the land and the intentions already in place there. The answer was yes. The bees would be a welcomed addition. We both did some reading on the subject, and Ellen went to the first two meetings of the Bee Keepers Association of Southern Maryland. We gathered our hives, painted them lavender, pink, and white and readied them for their new occupants who were on their way up from Georgia. We thought we were ready.

   Finally, on a cool overcast day, we picked up the bees at a farm about an hour from home. Three packages of bees weighed three pounds each. Excitedly, we carefully placed each package on top of its new home and went into the house to prepare the sugar water. Then, the comedy of errors began. We were following the directions demonstrated for us a month earlier by a local beekeeper. It seemed so simple at the time that we hadn't written anything down. We had to prepare the food for the bees before putting them into the hive. The sugar wouldn't dissolve in the cold water, but neither of us remembered the fellow saying anything about heating the water. Soon, we figured out that we needed to heat the water to have the sugar dissolve. (We've only been cooking for how long?) While it was cooling down, we decided to go to the store.

   By the time we got back, it was midday. What had been a cool cloudy day had suddenly turned sunny and hot just as we were attempting to place the first package of bees into the hive body. It wasn't working like the man or the book had said. The can of sugar water wouldn't slide out of the package, so we had to pry open the screen on the side. The queen, who is kept in a separate small cage, slipped down to the bottom of the hive as we tried to get the bees out of the screened package into the hive. The queen's cage was now down among the milling bees. We had to retrieve her in order to suspend her between the frames. With the increased heat of the day, the bees had become quite active. We had not covered ourselves or smoked the bees, because this was supposed to be an easy step one, two, and three process with docile bees happy to be in their new home.

---

[40]   Starhawk, *The Fifth Sacred Thing* (Bantam Books), 1994.

I got the rest of the bees into the hive body. Ellen retrieved the queen from the mass of moving bees. As she leaned over to replace the two additional frames, a number of angry bees flew up into her loose hair. She backed away immediately and tried to get them out with her hands. This movement made them even angrier. She was being stung repeatedly. Working as fast as I could to get the queen in place and the hive covered, I got stung as well, but not so badly. I was anxious to help her. I ran into the house to get my brush to see if I could get them out of her hair by brushing. By this time, Ellen was dancing around, crying out for help. What a scene!

A little later, we had quite a laugh at ourselves as we sat at the kitchen table, faces and scalps covered with white baking soda paste. We called her pharmacist husband, John, to bring some Benadryl when her stings began to swell considerably. This was turning into no laughing matter. Once all had calmed down, we realized that we still had two hives to fill with bees. We decided to ask for some guidance.

Ellen got quiet and called on Grandmother Oak to find out where we had gone wrong. The answer surprised us. We had been disrespectful. We didn't understand. What did she mean? We hadn't been afraid of the bees and had approached them with a lot of love as we welcomed them to their new home. But we hadn't taken in their side of the equation into account.

They had been uprooted from their home in Georgia the day before, brought eighteen hours north to LaPlata, and then brought another hour south to their new home today. They were disoriented and upset, especially as the heat of the sun had greeted them. We had not smoked them or covered ourselves. We expected them to feel the goodness in our hearts and accept us immediately. It takes time to build a relationship even with bees. Old legend has it that when a beekeeper dies, the new one must knock on the hive three times, announcing the death of the old keeper and his or her intention of taking over their care. Starhawk's Melissa certainly had a very special relationship with her bees. Why would we expect our bees to know us immediately?

We gave special thanks to Grandmother Oak for her sound advice, and the preparation of the last two hives went smoothly. We had only had these bees for a few hours, and already they were teaching us valuable lessons. As I go out to feed them now, I take the time to talk to them, admire their hard work, and express my gratitude for having them on this land!

2. Working with Other Forms of Intelligence

Information is made available to us from a variety of sources, like groups of ascended masters, saints, star beings, angels, animal helpers, devas, and nature spirits. We can receive information through a variety of means, like channeled readings, astrological birth chart interpretations, intuitive readings, and tarot cards readings. Information from these sources can sometimes be enormously helpful. Ultimately, it is really best to learn to move into the silence and develop our own personal way of tuning in to ourselves and multidimensional realities. If we choose to go for a reading by someone else, listen carefully. Is the information we are getting from the person who is doing the reading, or are we getting information from another source?

There are different levels of intelligence everywhere. What does the source sound, look, and/or feel like? Do you perceive integrity, love, respect, and caring? To be filled with the grace of God is to be filled with such an immensity of love that it is hard to contain it all. If you are being asked to do something that is not in your best interest or in the best interest of any other living thing on this planet or in this universe, then question the source and the information.

When other intelligences are being channeled, the person you are seeing in front of you is not the source of information, but serving as a vehicle for the transmission of information coming from another level of intelligence. The person in front of you may sound, look, or feel different from his/her normal self. One of the ways I recognize the Council of ADRON when my sister Starfeather is writing or speaking for them is that they use very poetic language filled with metaphors. My sister does not normally use language in this way. The pacing or rhythm of the council's speech is different, and her voice tones become somewhat lower.

Starfeather has done a lot of personal work to feel comfortable with them. It was very important to her that she and the council work in partnership. She is not subservient to them. They do not take control of her body. The Council of ADRON, who describes themselves as a group intelligence comprised of ascended masters and star beings, is apparently very excited about this particular experiment in a unique partnership, being experienced with for the first time. Over time, the work between Starfeather and the council has resulted in the "phone lines," as they like to say, between them being clear and open. When she prepares to open to the council, she takes great care to invite them respectfully to connect with her. Starfeather does this in a prayerful way, and then she takes her place at the council table as a member of a much larger team. This has taken a lot of practice, discipline, and trust on her part. When the Council of ADRON answers questions, you get the Council of ADRON and not Starfeather's ego mixed in.

Information comes to me differently. I will often get an image that is really more like a feeling than a clear picture. Or a place in my body, like my throat, will begin to close up and that physical reaction leads to new thoughts or feelings associated with the physical reaction. Reading my body's reaction to a question often results in surprising information as the words pour out relative to what I am feeling at the time. For example, one time, I was working with a friend and my throat began to get very tight. As I began to talk about feeling choked and not being allowed to speak out my own truth, she began to cry. I did not know until later that this was exactly what she was feeling and this issue was what needed healing. Another time, when I was doing a past-life therapy session,[41] I felt that we were in the desert. I could vaguely see a place much like Chaco Canyon. I trusted my feelings and directed the session to this place. My client responded immediately. This was obviously right for her as well. Sometimes pure energy that has no words at all attached to it moves through me. I have learned to simply let it flow and to trust that there is a purpose in it. Following my intuition, I make translations of this energy. Many times, there is an inner knowing that runs so deep there is no question in my mind about the truth of what is being given.

Machaelle Small Wright, in her work with the nature intelligences, teaches us how to get clear answers to yes/no questions by using the tool of kinesiology. This work is simple, clear, and very accessible. Pendulums can also be used in this manner. Her work is described in her books: *Flower Essences, Creating a Medical Assistance Team, Garden Workbooks I* and *II*, and *Co-Creative Science.*[42]

Knowledge coming from these resources is simply additional information you have gathered, with no guarantee that it is entirely accurate. It is one among many resources available to you. Always take time to check out your response. How does it fit for you? How does it feel? Don't give over your power. Discern what is best for you and develop your trust in it through practice and experience.

3. Discerning the True Voice

Eli Gatoga, of the Good Medicine Society, teaches us that we are now in the Age of the Coyote (the Aquarian Age). In past eras, we have been asked to "obey," then to "believe." Now, we have come to a time when we are asked to "know" by learning from our own experiences. No longer can we accept the truth from someone else. We must come to know that truth within ourselves. We are each being asked to carve our own way, and to know that we are not alone. We need to take what fits from the resources available to us and discard the rest.

How do you do such a thing?

Start with how the experience or the information feels, just like trying on a new suit of clothes. At first, the material may feel a little stiff, or the style may differ slightly from what you are use to. Sometimes you will know the moment you put it on that it's not for you. Other times, you will be intrigued as it brings out an aspect of yourself that has been hidden or laid dormant for many seasons.

---

[41]   Our patterns of behavior today can be often colored by trauma or experiences that we have carried forward from another lifetime. Past-life therapy helps the client access this information, gain insight from it, and release emotional attachment to these experiences. This work results in changes in the way we live our current lives.

[42]   *www.perelandra-ltd.com*

Or perhaps it's a whole new you that feels somehow right. Pay attention to the voices, feelings, and hunches inside of you. Don't let yourself be dominated by outside, external standards or expectations that you have set for yourself.

What is it that feels right? This is a little more complex than first meets the eye. When we are at our best, we have inner integrity. We fit congruently into the larger context. What we are doing and being is for the greater good of all created. Whatever we do, no matter how big or how small, is felt by the greater whole. Separateness is an illusion, a dream that we have come to believe. We have failed to see clearly our individual impact on the whole and are beginning now to see how our actions affect those who live downstream from us and those whose lives we touch. Everything we do, we speak, we think, we feel affects the whole universe.

If, as human beings, we use our conscious awareness to pay attention to the inner and interplay between others (all aspects of life), we become free to respond from the heart, fully present to the moment. Speaking and living our truth becomes our contribution to the ever-unfolding symphony of all of life. Living our truth may lead us to join the action on the front lines to change the way we walk with the earth, or it may lead us to work quietly in and near our homes to create the highest good for ourselves, our families, and our communities. The more sacred and prayerful our contributions, the more sacred and prayerful the whole becomes.

For this reason, it is essential that we learn to discern the voices that speak the truth inside and discard the old ones that bring us down and destroy us. Old fears tend to keep us stuck in old patterns of behavior that no longer serve us. They keep us chasing our tails out of fear of the new. Sometimes, we choose not to change the old patterns, even when we know that they are not very helpful, simply because they are familiar. In its familiarity, life is predictable, and that in and of itself is comforting. We have to be willing to let go of always knowing what is going to happen next in order to discover the beautiful surprises which life holds.

Sitting at the pray-place and soaking in the beauty of first light, I love the moment when the sun comes over the horizon. Even though it is still invisible to me, the sun illuminates the underside of the leaves with golden light. In the summer, I look at the many shades of green that shield the forest floor, listen intently for the sound of the little waterfalls in the brook at the bottom of the ravine and for the song of the wood thrush high in the trees above. In the winter, the deep shades of brown earth and bright blue sky are revealed to me. Cycles come and go as the winds play the music of the great harps of branches high above.

One night, our Holistic Healers Guild had an exhilarating meeting. Motivated by a soon-to-be-published medical directory, we began planning for our coming-out party. We had been meeting for over nine months, taking our time getting to know each other and each other's work. I had been nudging us toward becoming more public but had met resistance. Now the dam was opening up, and a free spontaneous flow of energy moved us toward making ourselves known to the community as a network of healers available to design and maintain a treatment team of complementary therapies for individuals in need of help. At this meeting, we designed an advertisement, a flyer, and an event that would introduce us to the community. The time felt right.

When our excitement subsided, talk shifted to the war in the Balkans and to the divisive role that the United States appeared to be playing. To see the chaotic truth emerge feels sometimes overwhelming to me. How can I as one person help with such an enormously complex problem? The night before, after some meditation, I had said to myself, "Well, I simply need to be impeccable. I need to stand clearly and strongly in loving presence, pray, and be the prayer. That is how I am available at this time to lend energy to the greater whole."

The next morning, at the pray-place, I was contemplating these feelings and noticed one lone pink lady slipper in glorious orchid bloom. It was bobbing gently up and down in the cool, dry winds of the early morning. It, too, must be experiencing the chaos in its own way. Spring had been unspeakably dry and cool, after very little snow and no rain since July a year ago. I found myself wondering about the flower. Had the lady slipper responded to the drought by diminishing its beauty? No, it stood as unique and spectacular as it had last spring. Bobbing slowly up and down on a cool, dry morning in mid-May, shining forth in all of its radiance, not really caring if anyone noticed it or not, the lovely flower was simply standing beautifully with no expectations. This affirmed my need to stand firm and strong in loving presence. What a lesson!

When I feel overwhelmed or out of sorts, I stop to tune into my own inner voice and to the guidance that is available around me. Often, signals from my intuition point me in the direction of questions I need to ask or information I need to seek out. Once I get the information, I try it on for size and see how it feels. What kind of results am I getting from these new ideas? If it feels life affirming and highly compatible with my energy, then I move forward accordingly. This is my way of discerning the true voice.

4. Being Too Naive

A while ago, Starfeather had a dream in which she was walking slowly down a ramp that was crossing over a small river. People were streaming past her. Someone very close to her asked her to hurry in order to get to the brilliant light toward which everyone else was rushing. Inside, she felt no pull toward the light. When she looked down to her right, she saw a huge old turtle covered with the deep mud of the streambed. They connected eye to eye and heart to heart. The turtle started walking in the opposite direction from the light. Starfeather felt much more at peace following the turtle.

How often are we compelled to follow the crowd without checking into our own inner feelings and hunches about the rightness of the action? Just because it is the "light" doesn't mean it is right or good for us. We need to come home to our own inner perceptions.

I have two clients who suffer from severe chronic depression. Both of them rail at the idea that they have created their present situation. One is a former schoolteacher, and the other used to be able to practice law. The lawyer, who is very bright and well trained, has developed a great deal of sensitivity to the issues of mental-health consumers. She longs for the day when she can again work in the field of law. Her disease robs her of energy, motivation, clarity of thought, and memory. She is at her best at 3 a.m., but it is hard to find a job that will accommodate those hours! Recently, another medication was added to her long list of medications. It has given her more positive energy. Her sleep patterns and ability to focus have shifted enough, so that now, she has a part-time job. She wants more, and it is a precarious beginning back to working full time as a lawyer.

The teacher carries many memories of the students that she took great delight in teaching. She fought leaving teaching for a long time because her work with disadvantaged children meant a great deal to her. Most of all today, she would like to have enough energy and concentration to complete the tasks of daily living. She would like to take a course in comparative religions, a subject that has always interested her, and she would like to volunteer with others concerned with environmental issues. She always has to stop and consider whether or not she will have enough energy or concentration to follow through.

Both the lawyer and the teacher are on medication, which sometimes works fairly well, but for an unpredictable period of time. They use the periods of time when they have energy and focus, but the lack of predictability and continuity makes it difficult to commit to jobs or projects.

There are people all over this planet who suffer from a wide range of afflictions and traumas. Do they call this reality to themselves? Does their soul or God, for that matter, call for this life experience? Thomas Merton was known to say that some people with mental retardation were highly evolved souls. Why not? We are not judge and jury, and neither is God.

We have an unconscious aspect of our mind that informs our present experience, sometimes in self-destructive ways. To face our dark side, to take responsibility for all of who we are, the yin/yang of our being, is to embark on a healing journey. We can make this journey out of a place of patience and loving kindness to ourselves. Fear and hate breed more fear and hate. There is no need to beat ourselves up for our inevitable imperfections. There is also no need to stay wallowing in our past muck and mire. This keeps us stuck in the past and prevents forward motion. By shining the *divine light* of love on the shame, releasing old destructive patterns of behavior, and forgiving ourselves and others, we begin to clear the path before us.

All the world is not sweetness and light. Ten thousand Nicaraguans died in floods caused by a hurricane. More died from the diseases that followed. A single earthquake devastated large portions of Turkey. There are many things, large and small, over which we have no control and for which we have no rational explanation. We can make the world a richer place by developing forgiveness, empathy, and compassion and by changing what we have the power to change in our own lives. By being in touch with our loving heart and following our truth, we learn where and how we are to serve the greater whole.

Alcoholics Anonymous offers a beautifully simple serenity prayer.

> God, Grant me the serenity
> to accept the things I cannot change,
> the courage to change the things I can,
> and the wisdom to know the difference.

We will continue to grow and change until we die, and death is simply another form of change. To live out of a place of the heart and prayer does not negate the intense suffering that is sometimes endured. To think naively that all is love and light or that we as individuals are all that counts will quickly move us toward disaster. Finding and paying attention to the God within and our own inner wisdom serve as good guiding lights. In this manner, life becomes a co-creative process. This does not mean that we won't make mistakes. Love yourself for being human and grow through the experience.

5. Creating a MAP Team

Machaelle Small Wright teaches us how to create a medical assistance program (MAP) team and how to use flower essences for our health and well-being. She also teaches us a science that works with nature as a partner to solve serious environmental problems that have been created by humans. Back in the early 1970s, she set up a nature experimental center to explore a co-creative partnership with nature. Nature holds the bigger picture of relatedness to the earth and the universe. Nature supports balance and harmony within that bigger picture.

Her work with nature in her garden led her to look at the human body, mind, and spirit as a garden. She discovered that some of the same principles used in creating a healthy garden could also be used to create a healthy human. Working with the MAP (medical assistance program) team, is to open an energy vortex or a coning. This is like connecting for a conference call with the entities that you need for assistance at that time. Here's the way I just now used it for myself:

I was feeling overwhelmed, off balance, and somewhat bent out of shape. I had a lot that I wanted to do and, of course, a limited number of hours in the day to do it. I was in a highly creative time, which means that I had a lot of ideas for wonderful things to do. I had a garden, a professional practice, friends, Good Medicine Society lessons I wanted to teach, another book emerging, and a desire to create more art, as well as a need to spend some very important time doing nothing but simply being. In summary, there was a lot on my plate.

So I found a quiet place, and talking out loud, I asked to open a vortex of energy or coning into which I called my MAP team. I requested connection with the Overlighting Deva of human healing (that angelic being, who holds the blueprint for human wholeness and health), and I waited just a short while until I felt her loving presence in my heart. If I was unsure about the connection, I could have tested with kinesology or a pendulum. I asked that Nature join us in order to ground the healing energy into my physical being and relate my healing to the balance and harmony of the whole. Whatever healing happens in me has an effect on the whole, as the whole also affects me. I wanted to be in good relationship with that whole. The whole is first the whole of myself, and second, the whole of my external environment all the way to include the universe. There is really no separation between inner and outer.

Again, I paused to ensure good connection. Usually, my whole being lights up with a smile when I feel Nature connect with me. Then, I asked that the representatives of the White Brotherhood, who work with me on personal healing, to be a part of this coning. The White Brotherhood are higher intelligences, ascended masters (both male and female, white, black, yellow, or red), who have been working with humans for a very long time, to help us develop our bodies, minds, and spirits toward higher consciousness. "White Brotherhood" was a name given to this group a very long time ago. Again, I paused to feel the connection. I placed my higher self, the template for the best I can be and the one who holds my soul's development toward oneness with *all there is*, into this energy vortex. I also brought in Red-Tailed Hawk in the east, Hummingbird in the south, Snake to the west, and Bear to the north. These are personal helpers who embody aspects of each of the four directions for me.

Now that the coning was constituted, I spoke to the group that I connected with as if I am on a conference call. "I am feeling out of sorts, out of balance, discombobulated. I am feeling as if there is so much to do and so little time. I want very much to be writing, and I am aware of old patterns of avoidance taking place. I am asking for help in releasing these old patterns, because I truly enjoy the writing and want to do it. And I want to write in a balanced way that is to include other things that are for pleasure, as well as the tasks that are necessary. The other day, I was bitten by a tick that has infected me with Lyme disease. I am grateful for the way in which you, my medical assistance team, are working with me to get the proper treatment, bringing my body back into balance and harmony. I have to admit that it feels a little scary, and I am not crazy about being on antibiotics. I am also very grateful to Western medicine for having a treatment that is so easy. I ask for your help to settle down, to center, and to clear my mind.

I would like to start writing today. Are there any flower essences that will support me at this time?"

I was given direction to take some flower essences. I used the Perelandra essences that have been developed by Machaelle Small Wright. There are other kinds as well. Today, I was given about twelve of these essences to take. They worked almost immediately to shift my energy from distraught and chaotic to peaceful and flowing. After taking the essences, I laid quietly for a while to let the MAP team continue to work with my energy. I sensed the shifts occurring in my being. When I felt complete, I closed the coning by thanking each of the participants as I disconnected from them. I felt much calmer and clearer, as if I can make good choices about what I can do and when to do them. The path felt open to begin writing again.

This process can be done any time that you have a need to bring yourself into a better place of balance and harmony. These are resources, which we can use to keep ourselves a well-tuned prayer. For much more detailed information about this specific process, please refer to two books by Machaelle Small Wright, *Flower Essences* and *Medical Assistance Program*.

6. Opening to Guidance

1. Guidance comes in many different forms. There is a lot of help available when we take the time to ask. *Let go of the expectations* concerning the form in which the guidance will come and *pay attention to what comes your way.*
2. Take the time to learn how to *enter into the silence* and *pay attention to your own inner voice and your intuition.* Always check out the guidance that you receive from others with your own experience and how it feels to you.
3. Pay attention to the inner and interplay between yourself and all aspects of life. Learn to *respond from the heart and be fully present* to the moment.
4. Accept the things you have no control over and work to change only what is in your power to change. Be open to *love yourself and grow through your experiences.*
5. Learn to create your own personal medical assistance team.

CHAPTER IX

Prayer through the Use of Ritual

Bless us O God
and these thy gifts of Anno Domini
two thousand:
> air wrapping its silky husk around us
> great sweeps of overhead blue
>> grasping horizons by the rims
> gold of the sun-flakes, scarlet-birded cedar
>> lilacs, cathedrals, blankets, and rain
>> orange peel and sandalwood,
porches rocking a million stars
the beach, and a salting of gulls on the air.
>> campfires and lonely
>> vast acres of mercy
that we are about to receive
from your goodness
> your
> greatness
through God whose millennium
>> lasts only a cry
>> before it is time for
>> the next Anno Domini
>> three thousand:
> Bless us O God
> and these thy gifts

Sr. Eileen Haugh[43]

1. Creating Rituals

Rituals are ways to mark important events, life passages, or other special times. Often we think of rituals as only things that happen in church. Just take a

---

[43] Roberts, *Prayers for a Thousand Years*, p. 91.

minute to think about all of the rituals you already do as a part of your year. Anniversary and birthday parties are examples. You may have personal rituals with which you open and close your day. There may be a certain sequence of things which you do before going to bed, like taking a shower, brushing and flossing your teeth, removing your make-up or shaving, putting cream on your face, opening your bed covers, slipping in, taking nice long deep breaths, reviewing your day and saying a prayer of thanksgiving. We can bring the sacred into these mundane rituals by being aware of what we are doing and how we are doing them. If we bring an attitude of gratefulness and contentment to these tasks, these tasks become part of the magic that we weave into our everyday lives.

Also, there is a whole array of rituals, which we identify more clearly as such, like weddings, christenings, and Sunday church, and solstice ceremonies. We can learn to create our own ceremonies in order to have them more personally meaningful. For instance, more and more people are creating their own wedding ceremonies. Weaving in the sacred into your life brings more meaning and joy. By creating beauty in your own life through living life as a prayer, you make a beautiful contribution to the universe.

During the winter months, I was spending time out at the pray-place as a part of my morning ritual. I came there in the early morning, smudged, and sat for a long time. Enjoying the beauty that surrounded me, I paid attention to the different shapes of tree bodies, the blanket of leaves gifted to the earth to keep her warm in winter months, the beautiful shape of her body, and the stars twinkling their last light of night through bare branches. I took some nice long deep breaths to clear out the internal me. Sometimes, I used my rattle and sang songs to greet the sun and the four directions. Sometimes, I played my drum in whatever way I was moved to do it, or I used a particular form that I have been taught. Sometimes, I danced and drummed at the same time. This varied, depending on how I was feeling that particular day.

During the winter months of 1998, there were rumors that the United States was considering war as an alternative to push some reality in which the politicians had an investment. This alternative never makes much sense to me, especially when I am sitting surrounded by such beauty. Why destroy the earth or humans or any form of life unnecessarily? One particular morning, I found myself humming into energy centers in my body and outside of my body. By opening a coning to my *earth healing* team, an energy vortex was created. The intention was set to create a column of golden light in order to radiate loving energy. This was to be sent to wherever it was needed.

An image of the Washington Monument as a huge acupuncture needle in the heart of the nation's capital came to me. If it could be seen that way, why not use it to stimulate the earth's energy and healing power? As a column of golden light, the monument might send a peaceful, healing energy and loving vibration out into the city of Washington for the higher good of all things, in whatever way that might be manifested. This image appealed to me, so I spent some time doing an energy-cleansing process developed by Machaelle Small Wright in order to release any negative energy held in the monument. To activate the energy centers within, above, and below the monument, I imagined it contained within my body as I toned and sang to each of the chakras (energy centers) as if the monument's and mine were one and the same.

Because many of our cities have similar structures, it occurred to me that they could be used in a similar manner, which would reinforce the net of beautiful, supportive light around our planet. Starfeather lives just outside of Seattle. She liked the idea of the Space Needle being used in this way and got some guidance to write an article in the paper to call all of the healers in the Seattle area. They were to gather at the Space Needle on the fourth of July at 7 p.m.

When we spent some time together late that spring, we talked about it and decided it might be interesting to do a similar ceremony at the Washington monument at the same time that she would be at the Space Needle. Because the monument is such a masculine presence and the Space Needle seems so feminine, we began to think that this might be a way to create even more balance and harmony from coast to coast. A sacred marriage between the two would be an exciting addition to the ceremony. We began to visualize a rainbow of light connecting the two of them serving as a very powerful healing force.

I made up the following flyer based on one she had already put out. The Seattle paper had also become interested in the ceremony, which she had proposed, and they had offered to give her some free publicity. On the East Coast, I simply sent out the flyer to people on my mailing list.

Washington Monument Activation
Ceremony
July 4, 10 PM

We are called to come together to co-create a ceremony for Earth Healing and Heart Center Expansion. A few months ago, I saw the Washington Monument and other tall structures in cities across the planet as acupuncture needles that could be activated and used to create a loving, healing resonance in our cities.

My sister Starfeather has called the healers of Seattle to meet her at the Space Needle on July 4th at 7 p.m., Pacific Time, to activate the Space Needle. Let us do the same here on the East Coast and create a rainbow bridge of loving, healing energy across this continent in a form of sacred marriage between the masculine and feminine forces.

We will connect with the Earth and activate an energy point deep within Her body with our intention, thus opening a place where her loving essence can be accessed. In this ceremony, we will be calling to the Divine Below to connect with the Divine Above to join together in balance. We will be also drawing the energy into our own bodies as we activate ourselves as conduits of the loving energy between God the Mother and God the Father. These energies will be blended and grounded in our own expanded heart centers and sent to the Space Needle in Seattle at the same time they will be sending it here. We will envision a rainbow of light connecting the two monuments and healing energy sent around the world.

Come on an adventure! Call if you want to car pool. We will be leaving my house at 3:30 p.m. Or meet us at the Northwest corner of the monument at 10 p.m. Remember Washington will be full of people watching the fireworks. It is recommended that you take the metro in from New Carrolton, early. For more information, call Claybasket (Carol Marcy).

So the flyer went out. We had an idea and an intention, but no ceremony as of yet. Several days before the fourth, I decided to do a shamanic journey and connect with the Tennessee Diviner. Dr. Felicitas Goodman,[44] an anthropologist, discovered that certain postures of figures in cave drawings and small figurines found at gravesites seemed to facilitate shamanic journeys. She and her students discovered that the Tennessee Diviner, a figurine originally found at ancient gravesites in Tennessee, could be consulted when creating a ritual or ceremony. In my journey, a number of elements emerged and took the shape of a possible ceremony.

When I shared them with Starfeather, she added the vow she had written earlier that spring, before we knew that there would be a sacred marriage in this ceremony. She thought that there should be crystals present. At first, I could not imagine how we could safely have them there. At the last minute, I consulted with Adam, who was coming to the ceremony. He had very recently been at the crystal mines in Arkansas. He was told to bring three. We couldn't understand why there weren't supposed to be four (one for each of the four directions). It turned out that another one of the women had had an impulse to bring her own crystal, which made up the fourth.

Starfeather had made up a flower-essence solution for everyone at the ceremony to support the energy bodies of everyone involved. My friend, Phebe, has been using essences a lot in her work as an acupuncturist, so I asked if she could bring a solution that might help support and stabilize us during the ceremony. More pieces of this ceremony came together after my original journey. It was truly co-created.

---

[44]   Felicitas D. Goodman, *Where the Spirits Ride the Wind* (Bloomington: Indiana University Press, 1990).

I have to admit that it was quite intimidating to know that we were to be at the Washington Monument on the fourth of July with thousands of other people who had come to see the fireworks. It felt overwhelming, as if we were heading into the eye of the storm. Would we be able to have access to the monument? Could we be inconspicuous enough so that we could do what we had come to do quietly and peacefully? Would it be totally chaotic? Would the fireworks be over by 10 p.m.? There were many questions and only one response. Our intention was set. We would go with the flow, and all would happen exactly as it should. We were not alone. There would be thousands of people there, as well as all of our unseen friends and supporters. Starfeather had received some information that we were twenty years ahead of our time. Perhaps this was a dress rehearsal for ceremonies to come.

I wrote the following to serve as a guide for the ceremony:

Ceremony done July 4, 1998

1. Meet those who have not carpooled at 10 p.m. at NW corner of monument and explain the ceremony and open a coning. Invite in the Overlighting Deva of the Earth, the Deva of the Washington Monument, the Overlighting Deva of Healing, Nature, the aspects of the White Brotherhood, who are working with us, and each person adds in his or her Higher Self. A Flower Essence preparation is offered to stabilize the work.

2. Going clockwise, lay a circle of cornmeal around the monument. Leave a group of people at each of the Four Directions around the monument. One member of each group has a rattle, and one has a crystal. Each group faces the monument, standing one behind the other. The person with the rattle calls in the power of the direction in which they are standing.

3. Facing the monument, toning or humming, touch the Earth. See, feel and connect with the energy center deep within Her under the monument and under ourselves. Place your hands in front of your root chakra, humming into it and the root chakra of the monument. Repeat at each of your chakras and envision the chakra in the monument as well.

4. Facing first to the North and then to each of the directions, gather energy up from the earth with the hands into the heart, then from the sky into the heart, then raising the right hand to the sky and the left to the earth draw the balanced energy of peace and love to the heart and give it out to the direction you are facing.

5. Facing the monument again, imagine it as a column of light that is vibrating with loving energy. See yourself standing in this

column of light. Recognize that you are standing with all of the Ascended Masters, Angelic Realms, your medicine helpers and spirit guides and your spiritual ancestral heritage. Imagine a rainbow of light emanating from the top of the monument and moving out across the continent to meet the rainbow of light emanating from the Space Needle. Turning to the northwest, stand as the groom looking toward your bride. Hold your left hand to your heart and say:

> "I am of one heart
> I hold the energy to dream the new dream
> I now create and focus on this graceful shift,
> opening channels to the highest dimension.
> With ancient wisdom I walk.
> I anchor the light in Sacred Union."

Corn meal and tobacco are offered as we complete the vow by saying, "WE DO!"

6.   Take time to both see and feel the rainbow of light emanating from the monument and yourself connecting to the West Coast and to those who stand as the bride at the Space Needle. Dream your biggest dream of Heaven on Earth. Close with "Mitakuye Oyasin," "all my relations," "amen" or whatever you prefer, and complete the circle by walking to the starting point. With everyone together, the coning is closed and gratitude expressed. Pemmican and cornmeal are eaten as celebratory food for the sacred marriage.

Pemmican and cornmeal are foods traditionally used by native people when they marry. I had ground the cornmeal from some Aztec blue-dent corn, which I had grown. The pemmican was a little different. Jan had reminded me that it was dried meat and berries ground together. Because I am a vegetarian, meat was not readily available in my refrigerator at the last minute. I remembered getting a grain version of pemmican from the health-food store a long time ago. Since *Joy of Cooking* didn't have a recipe, I had to make up my own. What I invented actually ended up tasting fairly good.

The most important part of this ceremony for me was the feeling it engendered. As I moved through the ritual touching each energy center, balancing the masculine and feminine, feeding the heart, and healing the inside and outside, I fell in love. I fell in love with the beauty of the monument itself, with the beauty of the trees surrounding the park, with the city extending beyond the park, with the country and planet beyond that, and with the universe beyond that.

As I drew this loving energy into myself, I fell in love with myself and then, in turn, gave it away, only to replenish it all again. The resources felt endless. My ability to tap into those resources, gather them to myself, and in turn give them all away, was somehow so extraordinary, so beautiful, and so joyful. By the time I turned to face the Space Needle, I was the groom, full of light, full of strength and beauty, as tall if not taller than the magnificent white obelisk at my back. I was ready to say that I was of one heart, filled with ancient wisdom and love. I was indeed anchoring the light in sacred union with my bride at the other end of this turtle continent.

The fireworks had ended about 9:35, and most of the people cleared out quickly. There were still some people around. Several came to join us. Some watched quietly, asking questions afterward, while others continued their conversations. The park police came out on their horses to clear people out of the park. None of it seemed to matter. The whole universe felt as if it was flowing exactly as it should. Everything was beautiful, even the sea of trash left by the fireworks crowd.

I spoke to Starfeather the next day. Sixteen people started in the south because there were lots of people at the north buying tickets to go up the Space Needle to watch the fireworks. In spite of the carnival atmosphere, they did the ceremony, first offering corn bread to the spirits of the land so that they would never go hungry and water so that they would never go thirsty. This simple gesture was very powerful. One inebriated gentleman came to talk, so one of the men in Starfeather's group took him under a nearby tree and spent time with him, rejoining the group later. They decided to go around to all four directions as a group, rather than split up into four groups. By the time they came to the north, some other people got out of the line for the Space Needle and joined in the ritual.

The next day, one of the women, who had been at the ceremony, reported that television coverage of the Seattle fireworks had continually panned back and forth between fireworks at the Space Needle and at the Washington Monument. They, too, had inadvertently helped to form the rainbow bridge between bride and bridegroom.

There are several things to notice about the forming of this particular ritual. First, it ended up being considerably complex and simple at the same time and very public. Rituals, which you create, can be very small and quiet, or very big and public. For example, if you made a simple ritual of offering food to the spirits of the land so that they would never go hungry and water so that they would never go thirsty, what power in that simple gesture.

Second, when you are creating your own rituals, notice how elements come together piecemeal. I brought in some parts, discussed them with Starfeather, who added other elements, which she had been thinking about. More got added at the last minute as I asked some of the participants to bring certain things, like crystals and flower essences. Ellen, following her own intuition, brought her own crystal, which became an important missing piece that she didn't know about ahead of time.

Third, being able to go with the flow of the moment helped. When we got to the monument, there were a whole lot of things that were out of our control. For example, we couldn't be up close to the monument, but that worked out fine. Ellen got hassled by the park police while she was waiting in the north for John to return, completing the cornmeal circle. Together, they quietly moved all of the blankets behind the snow fence and continued to do the ritual. Starfeather decided to start in the south because the north felt blocked in the beginning. The man who took the inebriated fellow aside apparently felt that speaking with him was an important reason why he had come to participate. Each of these things was a way of responding to the present moment and what was presented. There was no one right way to perform this ritual. We had never done it before. To think that we could do it perfectly, whatever that meant, was not an issue. To be in the flow with all that came together at that moment in time was what counted. A beauty that had integrity emerged. It was also curious that there seemed to be such an imperative to do it that year. Neither of us felt any pull to repeat the ritual the next Fourth of July, even though originally we had fully expected to do it every year.

2. Sacred Dance of Ecstasy

This is another ritual that I created, which also involved others. The intention was to access the continual flow of *divine light* and *love* and set up a column of loving energy to be available for wherever it was needed. The following form was inspired by the work of Gabriel Roth.[45] I wanted to carry her ideas further, deepening the connection to the sacred. I did a shamanic journey using the posture of the Tennessee Diviner. The use of postures as doorways to the Divine for guidance to facilitate healing, transformation, and divination is as old as humankind. The following form emerged from the journey I took.

Setting sacred space:

1. Gather everyone into a circle.
2. Have someone smudge people in the circle, by bathing each person in the smoke created from burning desert sage.
3. Give everyone an overview of what is going to happen.
4. Stand in the east.

---

[45]   Gabrielle, Roth, *Maps to Ecstasy: Teachings of an Urban Shaman* (California: Nataraj Publishing, 1989, 1997). *Sweat Your Prayers* (New York: Tarcher/Putnam, 1998).

5. Beginning in the east, lay down on the floor a path of corn meal around the circle of people.
6. State the intention of the dance out loud by dedicating the vortex of energy created by the dance to Grandmother Earth and to the co-creation of heaven on earth.
7. Invite everyone to use their breath and their bodies as instruments for peace and love.
8. Come inside the circle from the east.
9. Draw a small circle in the middle with a mix of corn and tobacco. Draw spokes out with tobacco to each of the four directions.
10. Open a coning with the *earth healing* team and the Tennessee Diviner. Call in the powers of each of the four directions.
11. Ask each participant to add his or her higher self to the coning and remind them to disconnect their higher self before they leave the dance.

The warm-up:

1. Begin the music, which has been prerecorded or is live.
2. Open the circle to allow freedom of movement
3. Breathe, stretch, and articulate fingers, wrists, and arms while circling, loosening, and swinging them.
4. Initiate movements from the breath as it is being moved in and out of the body.

The dance:

Spend about five minutes in each of the following activities. Play music that suits each pattern of movement. Give words to help create the kinetic image.

1. Create angular movements with the body by thinking about creating geometric forms that form the molecular structure of all life.
2. Find a point of balance and play with it by losing it and regaining it.
3. Move parts of your body or all of you in a sunwise (clockwise) direction. Imagine being the sun and radiating out the power and energy of the sun. See the planets circling around you.
4. Move in a moon-wise fashion (counterclockwise). Imagine being the reflective moon by giving back the energy given to you, reflecting back the beauty you see.
3. Weave a connection between the sun and the moon in the form of infinity. Move continuously in figure eights, imagining infinite possibilities.
4. Dance the spirals of your DNA, of all of energy and of creation.

Free improvisation:

1. Dance freely and openly with live drumming or recorded music, incorporating previously explored movement patterns.
2. Enjoy your body.
3. Be playful.
4. Interact with the space, other dancers, and the musicians. Crawl inside the music and lose yourself to the divine flow of *all there is.*

Closing the ritual:

1. Close by holding hands in a circle.
2. Pay attention to your body, mind, and spirit.
3. When you have sensed your own energy, feel the energy running through your hands and heart around the circle.
4. See the circle sending ripples of energy out into the room around you and further and further out in increasing concentric circles to include the universe.
5. Close the coning by expressing gratitude for all that is given and all that is received.
6. Release the higher-self connection.
7. Sing a closing song like, "The Circle Is Open."

Take this dance and make it your own. I use a variety of music or live drummers. Use music that is in tune with your intention. For me, most rock-and-roll music is not. Using really familiar dance music encourages the dancers to move in old familiar patterns. Music that is less familiar helps us explore our bodies and energies in new and different ways. Experiment and enjoy!

3. Other Rituals

> "The simple ritual
> of lighting a candle
> at an altar
> can infuse ordinary
> moments with sacred
> meaning."

Denise Linn[46]

---

[46]   Linn, p.19

A long time ago, when I was living in northern Vermont and creating dance pieces, I was enthralled with the idea of creating rituals, dance/music/word rituals. I would carefully arrange the elements and invite people to watch. One such piece was dedicated to the bear and was performed in a field on our land. I painted my face black on one side and white on the other. Galway Kinnell, a well-known contemporary poet, read his poem "The Bear" as I moved through a series of carefully laid-out gestures. When the dance piece was over, I felt empty. I could make up all of these wonderful rituals, involve others or not, but there was no sense of community, no sense of connection to anyone else but me and some ancient memory I carried. What was a ritual if it was devoid of a community and a context?

In ancient times, rituals were performed for very specific and important reasons. They insured that the sun would rise the next morning, that the yearly sun cycle would repeat itself, that the hunt would be successful, that the crops would grow, that healthy babies would be born, or that healing would occur. There were big rituals involving the whole community and small ones involving several people or an individual. These rituals were deeply rooted in tradition and were repeated by successive generations. Children grew up learning them by watching them and then participating in them.

Today we are faced with a challenge of a different sort. We are a culture devoid of community and sacred rituals supporting the activities of that community. Some find rituals in churches, some at family gatherings or special holidays. How can we bring rituals back into our lives in a meaningful and shared way? They can serve as a valuable vehicle for the prayers, which we are creating and living, and maybe they can be as simple as lighting a candle at an altar that carries a specific intention.

4. Creating and Using Ritual

1. Weaving rituals into our lives helps us to honor our connection to the sacred.
2. Rituals can be very simple or quite complex. Take time to mark important times in your day and big events in your life with ritual.
3. Rituals can be public or private, involving lots of people or just yourself.
4. Create rituals by following your intuition, using a journey or meditation or a prescribed text.
5. When performing a ritual, set an intention and allow yourself to respond to the moment, as well as the preset form you have devised.
6. Enjoy the rituals that are available to you in your community.

CHAPTER X

Making Yourself Available

Unfolding Your Own Myth

Who gets up early to discover the moment light begins?
Who finds us circling her, bewildered, like atoms?
Who comes to a spring thirsty
and sees the moon reflected in it?
Who, like Jacob blind with grief and age,
smells the shirt of his lost son
and can see again?
Who lets a bucket down and brings up
a flowing prophet? Or like Moses goes for fire
and finds what burns inside the sunrise?
Jesus slips into a house to escape enemies
and opens a door to the other world.
Solomon cuts open a fish, and there's a gold ring.
Omar storms in to kill the prophet
and leaves with blessings.
Chase a deer and end up everywhere!
An oyster opens his mouth to swallow one drop.
Now there is a pearl.
A vagrant wanders empty ruins.
Suddenly he is wealthy.

But don't be satisfied with stories, how things
have gone for others. Unfold
your own myth, without complicated explanation,
so everyone will understand the passage,
We have opened you.

> Start walking toward Shams. Your legs will get heavy
> and tired. Then comes the moment
> of feeling wings you have grown,
> lifting.

Rumi[47]

1. Living Your Life as a Prayer

Perhaps you begin to see that you have something very important to contribute to all of life. Your life is very powerful indeed, powerful in ways both subtle and beautiful. You have the power to discover who you are, to walk in your own truth, to relate to the world around you through a loving heart, and to contribute your uniqueness to your community and to the earth. You can choose to become an active, conscious, co-creative partner with all of life when you acknowledge the Divine within you.

Stop . . .

Close your eyes.

Take several long deep breaths.

Feel your body.

What are you most aware of at this moment? If there is discomfort or pain, breathe into it. Give that place in your body a voice or a sound. Let the message rise to the surface, coming into your conscious awareness. If you don't understand or nothing comes, stay with it a little longer.

Be patient with yourself.

Love yourself.

On the exhalation, make a humming sound. Take that sound to the place in your body that is bothering you, or feel the vibration throughout your whole body. Feel the fullness of your being.

Be respectful.

Allow yourself to feel.

Give a prayer of gratitude for the miracle of your body and for your beauty even if you don't think of yourself as beautiful. It is never too late to begin.

Honor yourself in a caring manner.

Breathe. Feel the pain, if there is any, transform as you choose to pay attention to it.

Pay attention to your mind.

If there is a lot of mind chatter, simply observe it. Release worry and guilt, if they don't serve you, by breathing into the places in your body where you hold

---

[47]   Coleman Barks and John Moyne, trans., *The Essential Rumi* (HarperCollins, 1995).

it or into the words that keep you bound. Take the time to shift the conversations in your mind to positive, self-affirming statements. Later, you might write these down to help to reinforce a loving attitude toward yourself. Hum.

Open your eyes.

Keep breathing deeply.

Notice the beauty around you. Look at the colors and shapes.

Listen to the sounds around you. Pay close attention to those sounds, as if you could breathe them in and out of your body.

Begin to pray out loud or silently. Slowly create a long list of all that you are grateful for. As you do this, breathe into your heart.

Feel your heart.

Feel the energy of your heart grow stronger and stronger. Imagine that you are an epicenter of waves of loving energy moving from your heart out into the room, the house, the yard, and stretching out into the universe.

Later, make the time in your schedule to go for long walks in a local park, across a field, in the woods, in the mountains, or along the ocean.

Stop.

Notice your breath and your feet. Come into contact with the earth underneath your feet, as if you were White Buffalo Calf Woman caressing the skin of the Mother with each step. If you live in the city, feel the earth under the cement and asphalt. Feel her strength and endurance. Notice the beauty around you. Look and listen carefully, connecting with what you see and hear.

Breathe your experience into your heart. Feel the gratitude well up inside as if your cup is overflowing. Be aware of the constant give and take between yourself and what is around you.

When you are at work, stop every now and then. Close your eyes and breathe long and deep breathes. Shift your awareness from your mind down into your body.

Pay attention to your body and your feelings. Be kind and gentle to yourself by taking long nurturing breaths into sore places or by simply feeling the joy of the air moving into your expanding lungs and out into your body.

Let your mind wander to a place on this earth that you love.

Be there.

Let yourself experience that place: the sounds, colors, texture, smell, and feel of it. Feel the joy you receive from being there. Feel the peace in your heart. Open your eyes. Keep your awareness connected to your heart as you look around you. Imagine that you are seeing what is in your office (or wherever you find yourself) for the very first time. Take it all in. Let the peaceful energy from your heart bathe this space in your office as if it could shift the energy there.

See yourself as an epicenter of loving energy. The waves of energy generated by your heart are gradually moving out into the space around you. You might want to get up and stretch or go for a short walk paying attention to your heart and your breathing the whole time.

Make a prayer of gratitude for all the abilities and strengths that you have to contribute to your job.

Return to the task at hand feeling full and renewed.

On your way home from work, if you have the option, take the back roads where you can enjoy the green trees and beauty of the earth, even if it does take five minutes longer. There might be a nice place to stop for a few minutes.

Get out of your car and walk on the earth. Feel the texture of the ground under your feet. Express your gratitude for all that stirs your heart.

When you come into your driveway, notice those things that you really enjoy about your home. When you walk through the front door, take the time to greet your family.

Get down to the level of your children's eyes and connect with them. Tell your children how glad you are to see them. Ask them about their day and stay to listen. Let them know how you are feeling. Do the same with your spouse. Be affectionate and available.

Take time to connect with your home and your pets. Eat your meal together as a family. Give thanks for your food and for your family. Leave the newspaper, Internet, and television until later . . . if ever. Take time to do something you personally enjoy.

Be creative.

You are in charge of your life. Create your living prayer in a way that is meaningful to you. At the same time, be as respectful and loving to others and the earth as you are to yourself. You and I are both a part of and the same as the whole universe. The loving energy we create affects ourselves, those human and nonhumans around us, and the universe as a whole.

Dance your own magnificence.

You can make a difference!

Go for it!

2. The Practice of Generosity

This book has presented you with a number of ideas on ways to wer sacred into your everyday life and to see yourself as an important par whole if not the whole itself. Body, mind, and spirit are players wit whole. You do not exist outside of the context of a greater whole, the and all of creation. The Aboriginal morning greeting prayer says it s "We gather here within you, this special group of your beings . . . we everything we do today, say today, and hear today be only in the highest for all of life and everywhere throughout the universe."

We are the one verse that is heard throughout all of creation be are intimately connected to, interrelated to, and not separate from all of Your heart opens the doorway to it all. Honor the Divine within which and within which we live. It is time to say, "I am available, for I acknowl

I express a prayer in every action I take, every word I speak, and every feeling I have. I have the power to be an active, intentional, co-creative healing force in this universe. I am choosing to consciously create the prayer that I am."

3. The Sacred Marriage Within

The masculine and feminine are beautiful and whole within me. I am one with all of life. I am actively creating a balance between the shadow and light within myself. Trust, respect, freedom, and intimacy peacefully coexist. I am an active, intentional, co-creative partner within the Divine in the ever unfolding of the present moment. This is what I have to offer you and all of life.

> I am inner beauty.*
> *I am action ever unfolding.*
> I am circular breath space.
> *I am the exhalation of Brahma.*
> I am juicy darkness.
> *I am the glory of the light.*
> I am the silver mirror.
> *I am the straight path.*
> I am the dancing spiral.
> *I fly to the center.*
> I emerge from below.
> *I am the eagle soaring.*
> I hold the seed in my belly.
> *I am the seed.*
> I suckle all of life.
> *I drink sweet milk.*
> I am sweet honey.
> *I am the honey bee.*
> I am the fragrant flower.
> *I reach out to touch.*
> I am enveloping softness.
> *I am steady firmness.*
> I move with the tides.
> *I run with wild horses.*
> I am the ground you run on.
> *I am the sky that touches your breast.*
> I am stars twinkling red and blue.
> *I am spiraling galaxies.*

The feminine voice begins, alternating lines with the masculine voice

I am night sky.
I am owl swooping through.
I am the branch onto which you alight.
I am the song in the dark.
I am patterns of moonlight.
I am dark shadows.
I call your name.
I breathe in your sweet smell.
I feel your sea of strength.
I see the light in your heart.
I taste your true spirit.
I speed the arrow to your heart.
I open my heart to you.
I plunge into your warm spring.
I open my body to you.
I offer you my soul.
I merge with your being
In ecstatic union.
We are one. We are different. We are whole. We are separate. We are
    All. We are one. We are boundless love.

VG